A GUIDE TO TAX
RESEARCH DATABASES

1990-1992 Research Methodologies
Committee of the American Taxation Association

Robert P. Crum
Editor and Committee Chairperson

ISBN No. 0-86539-077-0

CONTENTS

FOREWORD

Through their collective efforts and expertise, Professor Robert Crum and members of the American Taxation Association Committee on Research Methodologies have produced a monograph that serves as a valuable resource for individuals researching tax policy issues. *A Guide to Tax Research Databases*, together with the companion publication, *A Guide to Tax Research Methodologies*, provides a comprehensive reference source on research methodologies and databases that will benefit American Taxation Association members and their students.

The American Taxation Association gratefully acknowledges the KPMG Peat Marwick Foundation for its financial support in printing and distributing copies of the completed study to members of the Association.

Kenneth H. Heller
President, 1990-91

PREFACE

The Research Methodologies Committee's charge from Ken Heller, the 1990-91 American Taxation Association president, was to produce a scholarly report on databases that are available to individuals who are researching tax policy issues and to describe the methods for accessing such databases. Ed Schnee, the 1991-92 president, continued that charge. This monograph, *A Guide to Tax Research Databases* is the result of those efforts. It is, in effect, an extension of *A Guide to Tax Research Methodologies*, prepared by the prior Committee. The current project focuses on the databases to which such methodologies can be applied in researching tax policy issues.

Taken together, the companion volumes provide a fairly comprehensive reference source. Their purpose is to provide an introduction to the practice of tax policy research. Tax policy research is the marriage of a tax issue with a methodological design—the focus of the first volume. Empirical research designs require a third element, data—the focus of the second volume. Both take an applied perspective. They discuss the appropriateness of the methodological approaches or the databases for investigating particular tax issues and cite specific examples where they have been applied. Furthermore, they provide references to advanced-study sources for those seeking more in-depth exposure to the topics.

From an issue/design perspective, the companion volumes address: theoretical-analytical tax research, financial market-based tax research, behavioral-experimental tax research, and statistical issues. They cover the major individual taxpayer and tax preparer databases (Individual Tax Model, Individual SOI Panel, Canadian individual tax data, TCMP data, and IRS taxpayer and tax practitioner surveys), sources of corporate taxpayer data (Corporate Tax Files, Compustat and Canadian corporate tax data), and indexes that allow tax researchers to tap into other databases not traditionally used by accountants. In addition, the second volume includes a taxonomy for bringing issues, methodological designs and data together, observations regarding research directions and a listing of research funding sources. Burns, Reeder and Wittenbach have already addressed *Publication Opportunities for Tax Researchers* (1988) in another ATA project.

We are gratefull to the KPMG Peat Marwick Foundation for financially supporting this publication. We are indebted to the authors, Frances Ayres, Danny Hollingsworth, David LaRue, Suzanne Luttman, Alan Macnaughton, Robert Ricketts, Steven Rich and Adrianne Slaymaker, for giving of themselves to share their knowledge with the ATA membership. Other members of the Committee who contributed to the project by serving as reviewers are Katherine Schipper, Douglas Shackelford and Terry Shevlin. Thank you.

Robert P. Crum
KPMG Peat Marwick Faculty Fellow and
Associate Professor of Accounting
Penn State University

Chapter 1
Overview of Tax Policy Research Issues, Methods and Data

SECTION 1: A TAXONOMY

Robert P. Crum
Penn State University

Most approaches to tax research, except analytical modeling approaches, rely upon empirical observation. Among empirical approaches, experimental research relies upon data specifically generated for the study through treatment manipulation, and survey and case study research often rely upon data collected for the specific project. Other empirical approaches tend to look at associations between variables already generated, captured, and often aggregated into databases. While the strength of the experimental data is the control afforded in the laboratory or through carefully controlled field experiments and the coincident ability to infer causation, data from prepared databases are generally easier to obtain, cover more observations than would otherwise be practical or economical to obtain and are generally generated in the "real world" in which economic and behavioral phenomenon operate. Because these data are observed without experimental manipulation and in the absence of strict controls on intervening variables, (are *ex post* data for actual taxpayers, etc.) they, at best, provide circumstantial evidence about causality. In general, observations from prepared databases are high on external validity but low on internal validity. However, because of the practical difficulty of obtaining large populations and realistic contexts through experimentation and specialized surveys, tax researchers have often deemed it appropriate to use observations from these prepared databases. A review of academic tax journals such as *The Journal of the American Taxation Association* and *National Tax Journal* indicates that the majority of tax studies use these prepared databases. Because of their prominence in tax research, this guide focuses on such sources of observations.

In much the same way that experimental data is specific to a particular research question, specific databases tend to be appropriate for investigating particular issues using particular methods of analyses. Prepared data become useful only in the context of the particular tax issue being investigated and the methodology chosen to link the empirical observations to that issue. That is, the methodology is the investigative model for analyzing the data from a particular issue perspective. Therefore, the interrelationships between issue, method and data are at the forefront in empirical approaches to tax policy research. This chapter focuses on the "issue/method/database" intersection of tax policy research. Specifically, Table 1 classifies studies by data source (if any) within "issue/method cells." Novices may find this approach useful in understanding the breadth of tax research and for understanding the interrelationships between the separate chapters in the two *Guides* in this series. Because Table 1 is more comprehensive than the set of databases covered in the individual chapters, all researchers should find it useful as a reference to potential sources of data (over 90 data sources are identified). Experienced researchers may be able to identify "holes" in the table that present research opportunities. Although Table 1 is primarily a reference, Frances Ayres makes a few observations about potential future directions in tax policy research in the second section of this chapter.

Construction of the Table

Issues and Methods. Tax studies address one or more of four underlying general issues: 1) revenue generation, 2) equity and tax distribution, 3) neutrality and the effects of taxes on decision making/behavior, or 4) tax administration and compliance. Those studies classified as *revenue generation* focus on determining the amount of a taxpayer's payment/liability under a particular tax law, the amount of revenue generated by the law, the tax rate required to generate a specified amount of revenue, or the differences in any of the foregoing between two laws. Those studies addressing *equity and tax distribution* issues focus on what portion of the total tax burden is borne by an individual taxpayer or group of taxpayers relative to other individuals or groups. "Fairness" of the burden in terms of ability to pay (vertical equity) or the variance in the burdens of similarly situated taxpayers (horizontal equity) is a common focus. The tax as a percentage of income (effective tax rate) is often used as a measure of the tax burden. Those studies investigating *neutrality and the effects of taxes on decisions/behaviors* go beyond the amount of tax and its distribution, to focus on how differences in tax burdens reflected in the after-tax costs (prices) of goods, services and actions (e.g., charitable giving or saving) encourage or discourage their use relative to others and how the positions of producers or consumers of those goods, services and actions are made better or worse off relative to others. In short, these studies focus on the reallocation of resources due to the tax. Studies in the area of *tax administration and compliance* focus on those processes necessary to determine the correct amount of the tax and the reporting and collection of that amount. Therefore, they range through the process by which taxpayers and tax preparers learn the tax law and form attitudes about taxation, the litigation processes for arbitrating the application of the law, the administrative processes for monitoring compliance with the law, and the costs of the reporting, collection and administrative system. Several studies address more than one issue and are thus listed more than once.

Studies were classified by nine methodologies or approaches to addressing the tax issue: 1) survey, 2) case study, 3) factorial experimental, 4) experimental economics, 5) simulation, 6) cross-sectional analyses, 7) implied behavior and decision cues, 8) capital markets, and 9) economic (analytical) modeling. Although these classifications may not be all-inclusive and often overlap, they do provide quite a variety of approaches to tax issues and applications of prepared databases. *Surveys* ask taxpayers/decision makers about their attitudes/opinions, about their situations, or about their probable actions when faced with a given scenario. They differ from an experiment in that they usually do not elicit an action in response to variations in a treatment and lack an incentive for the subject. The line between

TABLE 1
Taxonomy of Tax Policy Research

	Revenue Generation	Equity and Tax Distribution	Neutrality, Effects on Decisions	Tax Administration and Compliance
Survey	**MIP,SCB,NIP,SSB,SSR, ISI**-Bakija & Steuerle (1991)*@ **TLW**-Pechman & Engelhardt (1990)	**SCF**-Collins & Wyckoff (1991) **SCF**-Fuji & Hawley (1988) **SCQ**-Hite & Roberts (1991) **TOS**-Internal Revenue Service (1987)ll2 **CFE**-Meng & Gillespie (1986) **SCQ**-Milliron (1985)l2 **BLS,ISI**-Rock (1984) **TOS**-Yankelovich, Skelly and White (1984)ll2	**SCQ**-Boskin (1967)l4 **SCF**-Collins & Wyckoff (1988) **ICM,CCD,GFE,MOD**-Ferris (1988) **GAL,NES,CAB,GSS,TFF**-Hewitt (1986) **ICM**-Hirsch & Rufolo (1986) **PRX**-Hite & Long (1982)l3 **PPS**-Hubbard (1985) **SOM,GVF**-Papke (1987) **SCQ**-Porcano (1987)l2 **CES**-Reece (1979) **NSP**-Schiff (1985) **TLW**-Tanzi (1987)	**TLW,CST,CFS**-Crum (1985)l2, ll3 **TOS**-Internal Revenue Service(1985)ll2 **TPS**-Internal Revenue Service (1987)ll2 **TPS**-Internal Revenue Service (1988)l2 **TPS**-Jackson & Milliron (1989)l2, ll2 **TPS**-Jackson, Milliron & Toy (1988)l2, ll2 **SCQ**-Milliron (1985)l2 **SCQ**-Slemrod & Sorum (1984) **TOS**-Yankelovich, Skelly and White (1984)ll2
Case Study		**CSL**-Verrecchia (1982)	**GSP**-Mead, Muraoka & Sorensen (1982)	
Factorial (laboratory) Experimental	**SPE**-Swenson (1988)l4		**SPE**-Swenson (1988)l4	**SPE**-Anderson, Marchant, Robinson & Schadewald (1990)l4 **SPE,TCM**-Madeo, Schepanski, & Uecker (1987)l2, ll2 **SPE**-Marchant, Robinson, Anderson & Schadewald (1991)l4

TABLE 1 (Continued)

	Revenue Generation	Equity and Tax Distribution	Neutrality, Effects on Decisions	Tax Administration and Compliance
				SPE-Reckers, Sanders, & Wyndelts (1991) SPE-Schepanski & Kelsey (1990)
Experimental Economics			SPE-Kachelmeier, Limberg, & Schadewald (1991)I4 SPE-King & Wallin (1990)I4 SPE-Meade (1990)I4 SPE-Swenson (1989)I4	SPE-Alm, McKee & Beck (1990) SPE-Anderson, Anderson, Helleloid, Joyce & Schadewald (1990)
Simulation	CPS,LCS-Adamache & Sloan (1985)I2 MNI-Aquirre & Shome (1988) TLW,CST,CFS-Crum (1985)I2, II3 CST,CFS-Crum (1991)II3 FRB,SCB,NIP-Crum & Lubich (1989) CCS,CTS-Douglas (1990)II4 ITM-Enis & Craig (1984)I5, II1 ITM-Enis & Craig (1990)I5 CST-Hreha & Silhan	ITM-Anderson (1985)I5 ITM-Anderson (1988)I5 SSA,CPS,ISI-Boskin, Kotlikoff, Puffert & Shoven (1987) ISI,CPS,ITM,CES,SCB-Brashares,Speyer &Carlson (1988) CST-Bruttomesso & Ketz (1982)II3 ITM-Craig & Enis (1990)I5 CST,CFS-Crum (1991)II3 CIR-Daly, Jung, Mercier & Schweitzer (1987)II4	CPS,LCS-Adamache & Sloan (1985)I2 CES,SCB,BEA,IRS Ballard, Shoven & Whalley (1985)II1 CST,CFS-Crum (1991)II3 ASD-Downs & Hendershott (1987)II1 CRS,CST,ASD,BEA-Downs & Tehranian (1988)II1 GSP-Dworin & Deakin (1983) ITM-Enis & Craig (1990)I5	CST,CFS-Crum (1991)II3 ITM-Pitt & Slemrod (1989)I5 CSL-Pollard & Copeland (1985)

TABLE 1 (Continued)

Revenue Generation	Equity and Tax Distribution	Neutrality, Effects on Decisions	Tax Administration and Compliance
(1986)	CFS-Davidson & Weil (1975)II3	SOM,GVF-Papke (1987)	
CSD-Murphy & Wolfson (1991)II4	ITM-Enis & Craig (1984)I5, II1	TSY,RSD,DIA,NRS,CFS, CST-Shevlin (1987)I3, II3	
ITM-Pierce (1989)I5	ITM-Enis & Craig (1990)I5	CST-Shevlin (1990)I3, II3	
CST-Schmidt (1986)II3	ITM-Feenburg & Poterba (1991)I6	CTS-Van Wart & Ruggeri (1990)II4	
ITM-Slemrod & Yitzhaki (1983)I5	ITM,NIP,FOF,FHL-Feldstein (1988)I5		
	SHE,RPS,CPS-Follain & Ling (1991)		
	CSD-Grady (1990a)II4		
	CSD-Grady (1990b)II4		
	CTS-Howard, Ruggeri & Van Wart (1991)II4		
	CST-Hreha & Silhan (1986)		
	ITM-Madeo & Madeo (1984)I5		
	CSD-Maslove (1989)II4		
	CSD-Morrison & Oderkirk (1991)II4		
	ITM-Pierce (1989)I5		
	ITM,PIR-Ricketts (1990)I5		
	CST-Schmidt (1986)II3		
	ITM-Slemrod & Yitzhaki (1983)I5		
	CSI,ATT,BIE,SOM,SCB-Swenson (1987)I2,II3		

TABLE 1 (Continued)

	Revenue Generation	Equity and Tax Distribution	Neutrality, Effects on Decisions	Tax Administration and Compliance
		CST-Thornton (1987)II4 ITM,CPS,SCF,NIP-Wallace, Wasylenko &Weiner (1991)II4		
Cross-Sectional Analysis	COG-Ladd & Bradbury (1988) CPS,SAB,SSR-Oustlay & Wheeler (1982) OEC-Stockfisch (1985) SGT,COG,ASD,DOC-Wheaton (1983)I2 CST-Shevlin & Porter (1992)II3	ITM-Anderson (1985)I5 CST,CFS,MOD,PRI-Bernard & Hayn(1986)II3 PIR-Christian & Frischman (1989)I6 CIR-Daly, Jung, Mercier & Schweitzer (1987)II4 TCM-Dubin & Henson (1988)II2 PIR,ITM-Dunbar & Nordhauser (1991) ITM-Long (1988)I6 CST-Omer, Molloy & Ziebart (1991)I3, II3 PIR-O'Neil & Thompson (1987)I5, I6 PIR-O'Neil & Thompson (1988)I6 VAL-Porcano (1986)I3 ITM,PIR-Ricketts (1990)I5 TSY,RSD,DIA,NRS,CFS, CST-Shelvin (1987)I3, II3	IRS-Altshuler (1988) CST-Bodie, Light, Morck & Taggatt (1984)II3 BBW,COG,SOG,COP, MOD-Capeci (1991) MTA-Cromwell (1991) CST,CAP,TRD-Eisner, Albert & Sullivan (1984)II3 CST-Friedman (1982)II3 ISI,CST,MOD-Guenther (1992) CST-Halperin & Lanen (1987)II3 ISI,PRX,CFS,CRS-Lewellen, Loderer & Martin (1987)I3 VAL,MOD-Lowenstein & McLure (1988) RHS-McCarty (1990) CST,S36-Mittelstaedt (1989)I3 CSI,ISI,PSI,SSI,CBP, SCB,SGT,TFF,COG, GVF- Morgan & Mutti (1985)II3	CSL-Burns & Groomer (1983)I2 ITM-Long & Caudhill (1987)I5 CSL-Pollard & Copeland (1985) CSL-Whittington & Whittington (1980)I2

TABLE 1 (Continued)

	Revenue Generation	Equity and Tax Distribution	Neutrality, Effects on Decisions	Tax Administration and Compliance
		CST-Shelvin (1990)I3, II3 CST,MOD,FRB-Shelvin (1991) CST-Stickney & McGee (1982)I3 CSI-Weiss (1979)II3 TAR,CST-Wilkie (1988)I3, II3 CST-Wilkie & Limberg (1990)I3 COG-Wiseman (1989) CST,CSI-Zimmerman (1983)I3, II3	CST,S36,BBP,CSI-Omer & Reiter (1991)II3 CSI-Pasurka (1984)II3 CST,FOF-Scholes, Wilson & Wolfson (1990)I3, II1 CST,DOL,DCA,CFS,S36-Thomas (1988)I3, II3 PGC,SPD,WSJ,CFS,S36-Thomas (1989)I3	TCM-Chang & Schultz (1990)II2 TCM-Clotfelter (1983)I2, II2 TCM-Feinstein (1991)II2 CSL-Kramer (1982) SPE,TCM-Madeo, Schepanski & Uecker (1987)I2, II2 ITM-Slemrod (1985)I5 TCM-Slemrod (1989)II2
Implied Behavior and Decision Cues (Regression Modeling)	CST-Hreha & Silhan (1986) ITM-Long & Gwartney (1987)I5 COG,COP,SOG-Preston & Ichniowski (1991) CST-Schmidt (1986)II3	ITM-Long & Gwartney (1987)I5	PIR-Broman (1989)I6 SCF-Collins & Wyckoff (1988) PIR-Feenberg & Skinner (1989)I6 CST,S36,CRS-Francis & Reiter (1987)II3 CIR-Glenday, Gupta & Pawlik (1986)II4 IRS-Joulfaian (1991) CIR,CTS,CFE-Kitchen & Dalton (1990)II4 CES-Reece (1979) ITM-Robinson (1990)I6 CST,FOF-Scholes, Wilson & Wolfson (1990)I3, II1	

TABLE 1 (Continued)

	Revenue Generation	Equity and Tax Distribution	Neutrality, Effects on Decisions	Tax Administration and Compliance
			TCM-Slemrod (1989)II2 CIR-Venti & Wise (1988)II4 SCB,FDI-Young (1988)	
Capital Markets Research		CRS,CST-Ayres (1987) CRS,CST-Courtenay, Crum & Keller (1989) MOD,NRS,BBT,CRS-Schipper, Thompson & Weil (1987)I3	UNS-Bathke, Rogers & Stern (1985)I2 CST,CRS,NRS-Biddle & Lindahl (1982)I3 CST-Bolster & Janjigian (1991)II1 BBW,COG,SOG,COP, MOD-Capeci (1991) CST,CRS,TAR-Cutler (1988)II1 CRS,CST,ASD,BEA-Downs & Tehranian (1988)II1 CRS,CST-Lyon (1989)II1 SBP,SOG,MOD-Metcalf (1991) KIS-Quigley & Rubinfeld (1991) CST,WSJ,SPD,DIS-Ricks (1982)I3 CRS or CST-Schipper & Thompson (1983)I3 NRS,CRS,DTR-Shaw (1988)I3 CGT-Slemrod (1982)	DTR,CRS,CFS,MOD,FDI-Madeo & Pinches (1985)I3

TABLE 1 (Continued)

	Revenue Generation	Equity and Tax Distribution	Neutrality, Effects on Decisions	Tax Administration and Compliance
Economic Modeling	**UNS**-Hendershott, Toder & Won (1991)	**NON**-Clotfelter (1979)I1 **SHE,RPS,CPS**-Follain & Ling (1991) **NON**-Mieszkowski (1969)I1	**SCQ**-Boskin (1967)I4 **NON**-Bulow & Summers (1984)I1 **NON**-Clotfelter (1979)I1 **NON**-Feldstein (1980)I1 **NON**-Fellingham & Wolfson (1985)I1, II1 **NON**-Fellingham & Young (1989)I1 **NON**-Halperin & Maindiratta (1989)I1 **NON**-Halperin & Srinidhi (1987)I1 **NON**-Halperin & Tzur (1985)I1 **UNS**-Hendershott, Toder & Won (1991) **NON**-Kau & Keenan (1983)I1 **NON**-Kolm (1973)I1 **NON**-Macnaughton (1992) **NON**-Mumy (1985)I1, II1 **ASD**-O'Neil, Saftner & Dillaway (1983) **NON**-Watson (1988)I1 **NON**-Wolfson (1985)I1	**NON**-Beck & Jung (1989a)I1 **NON**-Beck & Jung (1989b)I1 **NON**-Cowell & Gordon (1988) **NON**-Reiganum & Wilde (1985) **NON**-Srinivasan (1973)I1

* The citation entries followed by a Roman and Arabic numeral combination are cited either in *A Guide to Tax Research Methodologies* (ATA Section of AAA, 1991)—designated by the Roman "I"—or in this *A Guide to Tax Research Databases*—designated by the Roman "II." The Arabic numeral indicates the chapter number

TABLE 1 (Continued)

@   The three letter combinations preceding the citations refer to the following data sources:

ASD-   Assumed data
ATT-   Accounting Trends and Techniques
BBT-   Blue Book of Trucking Industry
BBP-   Blue Book of Pension Funds
BBW-   Bond Buyer's Post-Sale Worksheets
BEA-   Bureau of Economic Analysis Input-Output Matrix
BIE-   Bureau of Industrial Economics U.S. Industrial Outlook
BLS-   Bureau of Labor Statistics Handbook of Labor Statistics
CAB-   Survey of Consumer Attitude and Behavior (U. Mich. Survey Research Center)
CAP-   Capital Expenditure Survey (McGraw-Hill)
CBP-   County Business Patterns (Bureau of Census)
CCD-   County and City Databook
CCS-   Statistics Canada's Corporation Taxation Statistics, Corporation Financial Statistics, Fixed Capital Flows and Stocks, and National Income and Expenditure Accounts
CES-   Consumer Expenditure Survey (Bureau of Labor Statistics)
CFE-   Statistics Canada's Family Expenditure Survey
CFS-   Company Financial Statements or 10K filings
CGT-   1973 Capital gains transaction data from IRS
CIR-   Canadian income tax returns (Revenue Canada, Department of Finance)
COG-   Census of Governments (Bureau of Census)
COP-   Census of Population and Housing (Bureau of Census)
CPS-   Current Population Survey/Reports (Bureau of Census)
CRS-   CRSP tapes
CSD-   Canada's Social Policy Simulation Database and Model (SPSD/M)
CSI-   Corporate Statistics of Income (Corporate Source Book File)
CSL-   Case Litigation
CST-   Compustat
CTS-   Revenue Canada's Taxation Statistics
DCA-   Directory of Corporate Affiliates
DIA-   DIALOG Information Retrieval Services
DIS-   Disclosure Journal
DOC-   Department of Commerce data
DOL-   Department of Labor Form 5500 data

TABLE 1 (Continued)

DTR-	Daily Taxation and Accounting Reports (Bureau of National Affairs)
FDC-	Federal Deposit Insurance Corporation call reports
FDI-	Selected Data on Foreign Direct Investment in the U.S., 1950-79
FHL-	Federal Home Loan Bank Board interest rates
FOF-	Flow of Funds (Federal Reserve Board)
FRB-	Federal Reserve Bulletin
GAL-	Gallop Poll
GFE-	Annual Survey of Government Finance and Employment Statistics
GSP-	U.S. Geological Survey's Production and Revenue data
GSS-	General Social Surveys (U. Chicago National Opinion Research Center)
GVF-	Government Finances (Bureau of Census)
ICM-	International City Management Association Survey
IRS-	Confidential Treasury data
ISI-	Individual Statistics of Income (U.S. Treasury)
ITM-	Individual Tax Model
KIS-	Kenny Information Service bond trading data
LCS-	Department of Labor Compensation Surveys
MIP-	Money Income and Poverty Status in the United States (Bureau of Census)
MNI-	Mexican National Income discounts
MOD-	Moody's manuals (Industrial, Municipal, Government, Transportation, Bank & Finance, Bond Record, Tax Status of Dividends)
MTA-	Urban Mass Transportation Administration Annual Reports
NES-	American National Election Surveys (U. Mich. Survey Research Center)
NIP-	National Income and Product Accounts (Bureau of Economic Analysis)
NON-	No data
NRS-	NAARS (Mead Data)
NSP-	National Survey of Philanthropy
OEC-	Organization for Economic Cooperation and Development National Accounts
PGC-	Pension Guaranty Corporation list of reverted defined benefit plans
PIR-	Panel of Individual Returns
PPS-	U.S. President's Commision on Pension Policy Survey
PRI-	Price Indexes (Bureau of Labor Statistics)
PRX-	Proxy Statements
PSI-	Partnership Statistics of Income (U.S. Treasury)
RHS-	Retirement History Survey (Social Security Administration)

TABLE 1 (Continued)

RPS- Residential Mortgage Finance Panel Survey (National Association of Realtors)
RSD- Rudoff's Tax Shelter Directory
S36- SFAS-36 data tapes (Columbia U.)
SAB- Statistical Abstract of the U.S.
SBP- Annual Survey of Buying Power (Bill Communications)
SCB- Survey of Current Business (Bureau of Economic Analysis)
SCF- Survey of Consumer Finances (Federal Reserve Board)
SCQ- Self-Collected Questionnaire
SGT- State Government Tax Collections (Bureau of Census)
SHE- National Survey of Home Equity Loans (U. Michigan Survey Research Center)
SOG- Annual Survey of Governments (Bureau of Census)
SOM- Annual Survey of Manufacturers' (Bureau of Census)
SPD- Standard and Poor's Corporate Descriptors, Register or Million Dollar Directory
SPE- Self-Performed Experiment
SSA- Social Security Administration Actuarial Studies
SSB- Social Security [Administration] Bulletin Annual Statistical Supplement
SSI- Sole Proprietorship Statistics of Income (U.S. Treasury)
SSR- Social Security Administration Annual Report of Federal Old Age and Survivors Insurance and Disability Funds
TAR- Tax Analysts' Effective Corporate Tax Rates
TCM- Taxpayer Compliance Measurement Program (TCMP) data
TFF- Facts and Figures on Government Finance (Tax Foundation)
TLW- Tax laws
TOS- Taxpayer Opinion Survey
TPS- Tax Preparer Survey
TRD- Office of Tax Analysis dat aon R & D tax credits
TSY- Stranger's Tax Shelter Yearbook
UNS- Unspecified data source or various results from other studies
VAL- Value Line Data Base
WSJ- Wall Street Journal Index

surveys and experiments draws thin for those surveys that request responses to related but different scenarios. *Case studies* are in-depth analyses of one or a limited number of real tax situations. Experiments manipulate certain variables of interest while holding those not of interest constant. *Factorial (laboratory) experiments* systematically vary one or more stimulus variables for a single subject (or subject group) and measures the response to the variation in the stimulus. A distinction between these experiments and *experimental economics experiments* is that in experimental economics subjects are not acting in isolation but in competition with other subjects (i.e., in an economy). Thus, subjects may be acting strategically as well as in line with personal preferences. Factorial experiments tend to focus more on the cognitive process of responding while experimental economics tend to focus on the end result, i.e., obtaining the new equilibrium. *Simulations* are creations of data under assumptions about the distribution of derivative data and reactions to unobserved tax situations. Some are deterministic recalculations while others rely on random sampling from some assumed distribution of a variable. Often the assumed value or distribution is empirically derived from past observations. Simulations are used both to explore the distributions of variables under certain conditions and to test the conclusions of analytical models. *Cross-sectional analyses* investigate whether taxpayers with a certain trait (such as high capital intensity) also have other associated traits (such as different effective tax rates). Some studies (notably the LIFO/FIFO studies) calculate the probability of having a particular trait (LIFO) given the combination of other traits possessed by the subject. In such studies, the coefficients of the predictor traits (independent variables) are interpreted as the increase in probability that the subject will possess the object trait (dependent variable) from possession of the predictor trait. These studies are distinguished from the implied behavior and decision cues studies in that they fall short of inferring that the particular weighing (coefficients) of predictor traits determine the dependent variable. Studies which do infer how certain variables (traits or cues) are processed/combined to arrive at a decision or a behavioral response are classified as *implied behavior and decision cues*. Regression modeling is a common statistical tool for this research. The coefficients (when expressed as percentages) are interpreted as elasticities, i.e, the change in the dependent variable in response to the change in the independent variable. However, unlike experiments where stimuli are manipulated and other variables are controlled, data are often *ex post* in nature. Thus, the coincidence of variables of interest and the measurement and statistical control of other variables provides circumstantial evidence of the response to stimuli. *Capital markets* approaches focus on the receipt of the benefits or burdens of taxation by the owners of tax entities through the capital market's pricing of such benefits in the form of changes in (differences between) share (ownership) prices. To the extent that markets are efficient, the observed price changes are unbiased estimates, given the available information, of the incidence of the tax change on capital. *Economic (analytical) modeling* can be thought of as simulation free of data. Analytical modeling sets up the assumed relationships between variables and gives the properties of the solution, while simulation calculates the solution for a particular data set. As such, economic modeling relies upon mathematical properties to arrive at a prediction of the response to a stimulus rather than specific empirical interrelationships among data. The models are often the source of predictions made in developing hypotheses for empirical approaches and simulations.

Entries in the Table. Table 1 is intended to illustrate the extensive use of prepared data across tax issues and methodologies. Many more data sources are listed in the table than are covered in the two *Guides.* Studies not using prepared data are also listed to provide readers with a perspective of how prepared data contributes to the overall set of academic tax policy research and how studies using and not using prepared data corroborate each other, creating a mosaic of knowledge about tax policy.

Specific entries were determined according to the following criteria. First, studies used as illustrations in the two *Guides* are included. These entries are followed by a two-part symbol; the Roman numeral refers to the *Guide* and the Arabic numeral indicates the chapter which references the cited study. Second, tax and accounting journals were reviewed for prepared data sources not already represented in an "issue/method/data cell" and added to those cells. Third, where possible, at least three entries are listed per cell to give a "feel" for research in this cell. Finally, if a cell included studies with quite different specific tax subject areas, at least one from these different areas was listed. A more comprehensive table from which Table 1 was pared is available from the author.

Observations from the Table

Table 1 demonstrates the substantial extent to which pre-collected data are used in tax research and, through example, that tax researchers are often not as impeded for lack of data as might appear initially. Table 1 data sources are more extensive than those covered in this and the prior *Guide.* These *Guides* discuss those databases used most often by accounting tax researchers, but, as researchers, we should not be restricted to these. Economists have used prepared data more extensively than accountants, and we might learn from their applications. Researchers may consult the respective referenced articles for leads on these additional data sources.

There has been an increasing trend towards cross-over of accountants into economics journals such as *The National Tax Journal.* Within academic accounting, linkages also exist between financial and managerial accounting and tax issues related to managers' choices and the impact of financial reporting of taxes on decisions of various individuals. Thus, methodologies, issues and data span tax policy, financial economics, managerial decision making and financial reporting.

The same database is often used for different issues and with different methodologies, even within the same study, and many studies require multiple data sources. Depending on the level of analysis, these are merged directly or through formalized merging routines. Summary data for many of the sources are also reported in *Facts and Figures on Government Finance* (Tax Foundation) and *Statistical Abstracts of the United States* (Bureau of the Census, U.S. Department of Commerce). In addition to the table of issues/methods/data, readers may also want to consult other references. Burns and Gately have put together and periodically update *Tax Research: An Annotated Bibliography*, Brighton and Michaelsen (1985) profiled tax dissertations in accounting for 1967-1984 and O'Neil, Cathey and Flesher (1988) have analyzed differences in accounting and non-accounting tax dissertations for 1977-1985.

Relation to the Rest of the *Guide*

This chapter addresses tax policy research using a three dimensional matrix with the axes being issue, methodology and database. This triumvirate of 1) issue, 2) method and 3) data provides an overall framework for thinking about the ways that researchers have combined subsets of these three and for evaluating research opportunities. Hopefully, this approach will help the novice understand the possibilities for tax research, over and above the separate chapters on tax issues, methods and databases presented in *A Guide to Tax Research Methodologies* and *A Guide to Tax Research Databases*. The *Guides* cover the Individual Tax Model, Panel of Individual Returns, Compustat, Corporate Tax Files, Taxpayer Compliance Measurement Program (TCMP) data, The Taxpayer Survey, The Tax Practitioner Survey, Canadian Individual and Corporate return data and how to find other prepared data. Table 1 is intended as an overview and provides a reference list for data sources not covered in detail.

SECTION 2: FUTURE DIRECTIONS IN TAX POLICY RESEARCH

Frances L. Ayres
The University of Oklahoma

This section broadly examines the area of tax policy focusing on areas where additional research is needed. This section is restricted in several respects. First, the focus is on areas where empirical research could be conducted using existing archival databases. This does not imply that important questions cannot be addressed using alternative methods including analytical modeling and experimental methodology. In fact, in many areas, research using combinations of empirical, analytical and experimental work is needed. However, this committee focused on available archival databases and research addressable using this data. Second, we seek to focus on areas where academic tax accountants may have a competitive advantage over individuals in economics and finance who often lack strong institutional knowledge of the details of tax practice and law. While many of the important issues have been addressed in both economics and finance, in many cases their conclusions are limited because of simplifying assumptions made about how particular policies are implemented. Third, the Scholes/Wolfson (1992) framework is not discussed separately here. The reader is referred to recent comments by Wilson (1991) regarding tax research following this direction. Many of the databases described in the taxonomy section are potentially useful in empirical tests of the Scholes/Wolfson framework.

Databases which are available are listed in Table 1 of the taxonomy section. The available data bases include fairly detailed information about publicly traded corporations at the individual firm and industry level, and more limited information on individuals. Critical tax policy questions which are in need of addressing fall into both areas.

The remainder of this section poses a series of unanswered questions in corporate and personal tax policy which are addressable using empirical method and archival databases.

Corporate Tax Data and Research Questions:

1) What is the relation between security returns and changes in tax policy? This question, while broad in scope, is of critical importance to policymakers. The importance of stock market reactions to tax disclosures and tax policy changes has become an emerging area of work to researchers in accounting, finance and economics. Recent economic research has examined both theoretical and empirical questions relating to the impact of tax changes on equity stock prices. (For examples see Cutler (1988), Downs and Tehranian (1988), Lyon (1989), and Bolster and Janjigian (1991), and Downs and Hendershott (1987).) Questions that have been addressed relating to this issue cover topics in the areas of equity, neutrality, incidence and administration and compliance.

Particularly in the corporate area, much of tax policy seems to encourage investment in targeted areas vis a vis differential taxation. For example, the investment tax credit was designed to encourage investment in real assets by providing a direct credit against taxes due for firms investing in qualified assets. The research and development tax credit serves a similar function for investment in qualified research and development activities. There are also numerous areas where specialized taxes have been directed at a particular industry, such as the oil industry. Examples are the windfall profits tax, and specialized rules regarding percentage depletion.

One method of examining the effects of such specialized tax laws is to test for the impact of changes and anticipated changes in the law of the security prices of affected firms. In general, we expect that when a tax policy change is enacted which differentially affects selected corporations the capital market will respond. Such revaluation effects can be captured through either unexpected returns estimated from the well-known market model, or through changes in systematic risk or beta. Omer and Shaw (1991) discuss methodological difficulties in applying capital markets research to the tax area in some depth. Hence no attempt is made here to provide a detailed analysis of these issues. However several points merit emphasis.

First, an important caveat to this line of research is that any analysis that is done is a partial equilibrium model. As such, the overall impact of more broad-based tax policy changes is much more difficult to test, and is more appropriately examined using analytical modeling techniques. Capital markets techniques can be used to test for the differential effects across firms of tax policy changes.

For example, suppose that a researcher was interested in the capital market impact of the *Tax Reform Act of 1986*. The overall affect of the *Act* on security values would not be testable using the capital markets methodology because any effect that occurred across all firms would be captured in the market impact. However, the *differential* capital market impact could be tested if the researcher had reason to believe that not all firms were equally affected. In this latter case, the reallocation across firms on the variable of interest could be examined through testing unexpected returns and/or risk shifts depending on the research question. Cutler (1988) and Bolster and Janjigian (1991) provide two examples of studies which examine the different aspects of the impact of the 1986 reform act.

Second, care should be taken in the statistical methods used. The researcher must take care to examine the data for the existence of significant cross-correlation in the returns of the sample firms. Because tax laws generally change in calendar time rather than event time, sample firms are being tested at the same point in time. Omer and Shaw (1991) discuss models that have been employed to address this problem.

Third, it is important that researchers carefully consider the assumptions underlying the model tested. The question of "who benefits" from tax policy changes is not always clear-cut. In some cases alternative theories exist which may lead to conflicting predictions (see for example, Lyon (1989)).

The data to be used for this type of methodology vary. However, the dependent variable would generally be the unexpected returns obtained from the CRSP tapes. The independent variables would depend upon the question addressed by the researcher. For example, if there was reason to believe that the *Tax Reform Act* had a differential effect on firms with different types of capital structure then the appropriate independent variables would include firm-specific measure of capital structure. The particular research designs vary and could include grouping by variables of interest and testing for differential returns across groups, or if the independent variables are continuous, using cross-sectional regressions. Sources of firm-specific information that can be used as independent variables vary, but include NAARS, Compustat, Proxy Statements and others.

The aforementioned databases have been mined rather heavily by researchers in finance and accounting. An area that has been less addressed is firm-specific data from actual tax returns. Such data may be obtainable from the IRS for selected firms. Aggregate corporate data is available from the Statistics of Income Database. Detailed data from corporate tax returns are proprietary and available only to IRS employees. A faculty member may take a leave of absence and be employed by the IRS in order to obtain access to the data.

Examples of capital market research in addition to those cited here are listed in the Taxonomy. Although there has been a fair amount of research in the area, many questions remain unanswered. In the financial accounting area there have been over 200 published studies addressing the capital market impact of various accounting disclosures. In sharp contrast empirical tax researchers have only begun to scratch the surface in this area.

An issue related to the impact of corporate tax changes on equity values is the impact of corporate tax changes on bond markets. There has been little research addressing questions of how and to what extent tax changes affect bond prices. This is likely due to the relative difficulty in accessing data and the lack of theoretical models of bond prices. However, there have been a limited number of studies in finance and accounting regarding the impact on bond prices of accounting disclosures such as earnings. This suggests that examining the impact of tax law changes on bond markets may also be a fruitful area of research.

2) How do changes in corporate taxes affect tax revenues? This is an area which has received considerably less attention than the capital markets area in corporate tax. Yet it remains of critical importance to policymakers. We found no examples of attempts to examine revenue effect using the capital markets methodology. This is because capital markets methodology provides no direct measure of how a particular tax policy impacts revenues. However, the capital market impact of tax changes would have an important impact on revenues in that if one group of firms is positively impacted relative to another in the market, then the revenues from the former would be expected to increase to the extent that the increased cash flows led to increased taxable income. More research is needed to examine the linkage between capital market behavior and revenue estimation. The design of this type of study would be difficult because it would need to incorporate a method of linking capital markets effects to changes in future revenues. This is a relatively unexplored area.

A possible method is to combine methodologies such as simulation, experimental markets and analytical modeling with empirical studies based on actual capital markets data. The majority of revenue estimation studies to date take the form of simulations, cross-sectional analyses of taxes paid by segments and to a lesser extent, economic modeling. Numerous examples are provided in the Taxonomy under the "Revenue Generation" subheading. A useful area of future research would be to link one or more of these methodologies with tests of capital market effects.

3) Where does the corporate tax burden fall? A number of important issues fall under this general question. The previously discussed capital markets methodology provides one means to test for differences across equity returns caused by tax policy changes. However, other methods include attempts to directly test for differences in the tax burden across firms and industry. Compustat provides data which can be used to measure effective tax rates across different industries. Simulation has been used in a number of studies to test for differences in tax burdens. Much of this relates to the revenue estimation area. Examples of research relating to the distribution of the tax burden are provided in the Taxonomy under the subheading of "Equity and Tax Distribution."

4) How do corporate managers structure decisions to consider tax consequences? There has been little research addressing issues relating to the behavior of corporate managers in response to taxation. One approach to address this issue is analytical modeling and resulting analytical predictions could be followed by experimental markets verifications. However, a shortcoming of this type of research is the unrealistic assumptions often made about how the world works. A possible fruitful approach to learn more about how managers deal with taxes would be in-depth case studies, and possibly survey research. Another approach is to use archival data such as Compustat and attempt to infer managers' behavior about taxes from observations about corporate structure changes and other changes in the financial statements. For example, firms which become more profitable would be expected to show increased concern about taxes and to engage to a greater extent in tax minimizing behavior. This effect has been shown in the LIFO/FIFO area. However, few other types of decisions have been analyzed. Examples of research examining the impact of taxes on managers' decisions include Scholes, Wilson and Wolfson (1990), Mumy (1985), and Fellingham and Wolfson (1985). Other examples can be found in the Taxonomy under the subcategory of "Neutrality and the Effect (of Taxes) on Decisions."

In summary, a large amount of archival data exists which can be mined to address critical questions related to corporate tax policy. While there has been a fair amount of research in the area, many questions remain unanswered. Direct empirical research at the micro-level of corporate tax policy issues is a relatively recent phenomena. In part this has been due to changes in disclosure requirements and in part due to a shift in the type of research conducted by accountants in the tax area. Traditional research in economics and finance relies heavily on analytical modeling and aggregate databases. Academic accountants trained in the tax area are well-positioned to fill this necessary void.

Personal Income Tax Questions:

Many of the same questions related to corporate taxes also apply to the personal income tax. In addition, a number of additional issues relating to individual behavior and tax compliance exist.

1) How do changes in personal taxes affect security returns? This is a difficult question to address using traditional capital market methods. The problem is that while changes in personal taxes have an effect on bond and equity markets much of the effect will be captured in the market indices. In order to examine the extent to which personal tax changes affect equity and bond values it is necessary to either employ a general equilibrium model with aggregate prices, or to find subsets of firms for which ownership structure differs (clientele effects) and examine the impact of personal tax changes across firms which have different types of holdings. For example, firms which are primarily held by institutions may respond differently to changes in personal taxes than widely held firms. A recent example is Bolster and Janjigian (1991) who examined the valuation impact of the *Tax Reform Act of 1986* as a function of firms' dividend policy.

2) What is the revenue impact of changes in the rate and type of personal tax? This question has been addressed using simulation and analytical methodology, cross-sectional studies and to a lesser extent experimental markets. However, much work remains in this area. In part the problem is that most studies are partial equilibrium models which fail to account for changes in individual behavior in response to tax changes. Improved models of revenue estimation are needed for budgetary purposes and to improve our understanding of the impact of tax changes. Examples of this type of research are given under the "Revenue Generation" subcategory in the Taxonomy.

3) How is the individual tax burden distributed? The relative progressivity of individual taxes remains an important question. This has been addressed using survey methods to capture perceptions of equity. The most common method of addressing this issue has been through various cross-sectional models of relative taxes across individuals. However, questions remain. Particularly important are the interrelation of various taxes including property, income, social security, state taxes and sales taxes paid by individuals. A number of studies have addressed various combinations of these but the research which integrates various taxes and their burden on individuals is limited. Examples of research examining the overall tax burden are Enis and Craig (1984) and Ballard, Shoven and Whalley (1985). Other examples can be found under the "Equity and Tax Distribution" subheadings in the Taxonomy.

4) What is the cost of noncompliance and how can compliance be increased? A number of studies have addressed tax compliance issues. The methodologies are as varied as the questions addressed. There have been numerous survey and experimental studies which have attempted to determine the factors which influence compliance. One problem in determining the extent of noncompliance is that there is not general agreement as to what tax compliance is. A number of areas of tax law are ambiguous leading to an unclear definition of what a "compliant" position is. Research in the area has addressed both the role of the individual taxpayer and the paid tax preparer. The interrelationship between complexity and compliance has also been addressed to some extent. There has been limited research in the compliance area using the IRS panel data. However, direct evidence of noncompliance is difficult to obtain because of the confidentiality of individual returns. As a result, the compliance area has relied heavily on experimental and analytical methods. More research is needed to determine more precisely the population of noncompliant taxpayers and the cost of noncompliance to society. Numerous examples of tax compliance research are given in the Taxonomy under the category "Tax Administration and Compliance."

5) How effective are tax rate changes and specialized incentives in altering taxpayer behavior? Questions in this area relate to issues such as the level of retirement savings, charitable contributions, borrowing behavior, insurance and other areas where the government has sought to use the tax system to encourage or discourage certain behavior. Examples of this line of research fall primarily under the area of "Implied Behavior and Decision Cues" in the Taxonomy. Data for this type of research varies and is often difficult to obtain and/or proprietary. Sources include the Survey of Consumer Finances (SCF), the IRS panel data, and the Individual Tax Model among others. Unfortunately, the individual taxpayer data are limited to items that can be gleaned from the tax return. Possibilities for overcoming this hurdle include data merging (Luttman, 1990) and use of the more-detailed Canadian data discussed in Chapter 4.

6) How do other (non-income) taxes affect individual decisions? This relates to item (3) above. However, such issues are also examined separately in some cases. Examples of questions in this area include 1) What is the impact of changes in the corporate tax rate on investment decisions? 2) How do allocations of property tax affect taxpayer behavior? 3) What impact do changes in Social Security taxes have on retirement savings? 4) To what extent do tariffs discourage targeted economic activities? 5) How do different taxes affect the facilities location decision? Again, most of the data available in this area is aggregate data, as much of the data on individuals is proprietary. Greater availability of data in a disaggregate form could facilitate more research in this area. Examples of research in this area are primarily in the Survey and the Experimental methods sections.

The purpose of this section has been to point out some areas where research has been conducted using available databases and to point out some areas where future research is needed. Users interested in a particular area may refer to the examples in the Taxonomy. By pointing to some areas where questions need to be addressed, and providing examples of papers and the related data we hope to encourage future research to address many of these issues.

REFERENCES

Adamache, K. W., and F. A. Sloan. 1985. Fringe Benefits: To Tax or Not to Tax? *National Tax Journal* (March): 47-64.

Alm, J., M. McKee, and W. Beck. 1990. Amazing Grace: Tax Amnesties and Compliance. *National Tax Journal* (March): 23-37.

Altshuler, R. 1988. A Dynamic Analysis of the Research and Experimentation Credit. *National Tax Journal* (December): 453-466.

Anderson, K. 1985. A Horizontal Equity Analysis of the Minimum Tax Provisions: An Empirical Study. *The Accounting Review* (July): 351-371.

———. 1988. A Horizontal Equity Analysis of the Minimum Tax Provisions: 1976-1986 Tax Acts. *Journal of the American Taxation Association* (Fall): 7-25.

Anderson, M., U. Anderson, R. Helleloid, E. Joyce, and M. Schadewald. 1990. Internal Revenue Service Access to Tax Accrual Workpapers: A Laboratory Investigation. *The Accounting Review* (October): 857-874.

Anderson, U., G. Marchant, J. Robinson, and M. Schadewald. 1990. Selection of Instructional Strategies in the Presence of Related Prior Knowledge. *Issues in Accounting Education* (Spring): 41-58.

Aquirre, C. A., and P. Shome. 1988. The Mexican Value-Added Tax (VAT): Methodology for Calculating the Base, *National Tax Journal* (December): 543-554.

Ayres, F. L. 1987. An Empirical Assessment of the Effects of the Investment Tax Credit Legislation on Returns to Equity Securities. *Journal of Accounting and Public Policy* (Summer): 115-137.

Bakija, J., and E. Steuerle. 1991. Individual Income Taxation Since 1948. *National Tax Journal* (December): 451-475.

Ballard, C. L., J. B. Shoven, and J. Whalley. 1985. The Total Welfare Cost of the United States Tax System: A General Equilibrium Approach. *National Tax Journal* (June): 125-140.

Bathke, A. W. Jr., R. L. Rogers, and J. J. Stern. 1985. The Security Market Reaction to Tax Legislation as Reflected in Bond Price Adjustments. *Journal of the American Taxation Association* (Spring): 37-49.

Beck P. J., and W. Jung. 1989a. Taxpayers' Reporting Decisions and Auditing under Information Asymmetry. *The Accounting Review* (July): 468-487.

——— and ———. 1989b. Taxpayer Compliance under Uncertainty. *Journal of Accounting and Public Policy* (Spring): 1-29.

Bernard, V., and C. Hayn. 1986. Inflation and the Distribution of the Corporate Income Tax Burden. *National Tax Journal* (June): 172-187.

Biddle, G. C., and F. W. Lindahl. 1982. Stock Prices Reactions to LIFO Adoptions: The Association between Excess Returns and LIFO Tax Savings, *Journal of Accounting Research* (Autumn): 551-588.

Bodie, Z., J. O. Light, R. Morck, and R. A. Taggart, Jr. 1984. Funding and Asset Allocation in Corporate Pension Plans: An Empirical Investigation. Working Paper No. 1315. (National Bureau of Economic Research).

Bolster, P. J., and V. Janjigian. 1991. Dividend Policy and Valuation Effects of the Tax Reform Act of 1986. *National Tax Journal* (December): 511-518.

Boskin, M. 1967. The Negative Income Tax and the Supply of Work Effort. *National Tax Journal* (December): 353-367.

——, L. J. Kotlikoff, D. J. Puffert, and J. B. Shoven. 1987. Social Securiity: A Financial Appraisal Across and Within Generations. *National Tax Journal* (March): 19-34.

Brashares, E., J. F. Speyrer, and G. N. Carlson. 1988. Distributional Aspects of a Federal Value-Added Tax. *National Tax Journal* (June): 155-74.

Brighton, G. D., and R. H. Michaelsen. 1985. Profile of Tax Dissertations in Accounting: 1967-1984. *Journal of the American Taxation Association* (Spring): 76-91.

Broman, A. 1989. Statutory Tax Rate Reform and Charitable Contributions: Evidence from a Recent Period of Reform. *Journal of the American Taxation Association* (Fall): 7-21.

Bruttomesso, R. I., and J. E. Ketz. 1982. Historical Cost and General Price Level Tax Rates in Seven Industires. *Journal of the American Taxation Association* (Winter): 30- 36.

Bulow, J. I., and L. H. Summers. 1984. The Taxation of Risky Assets. *Journal of Political Economy* (February): 20-39.

Burns, J. O., and S. M. Groomer. 1983. An Analysis of Tax Court Decisions that Assess the Profit Motive of Farm-Oriented Operations. *Journal of the American Taxation Association* (Fall): 23-39.

——, and M. S. Gately. Periodically updated. *Tax Research: An Annotated Bibliography* (Texas Tach University).

Capeci, J. 1991. Credit Risk, Credit Ratings, and Municipal Bond Yields: A Panel Study. *National Tax Journal* (December): 41-56.

Chang, O., and J. J. Schultz. 1990. The Income Tax Withholding Phenomenom: Evidence from TCMP Data. *Journal of the American Taxation Association* (Fall): 88-92.

Christian, C. W., and P. J. Frischman. 1989. Attrition in the Statistics of Income Panel of Individual Returns. *National Tax Journal* (December): 495-501.

Clotfelter, C. T. 1979. Equity, Efficiency and the Tax Treatment of In-Kind Compensation. *National Tax Journal* (March): 51-60.

——. 1983. Tax Evasion and Tax Rates: An Analysis of Individual Returns. *Review of Economics and Statistics* (August): 363-373.

Collins, J. H., and J. H. Wyckoff. 1988. Estimates of Tax-Deferred Retirement Savings Behavior. *National Tax Journal* (December): 561-572.

—— and ——. 1991. Another Look at the Tax-Favored Retirement Savings Puzzle. *Journal of the American Taxation Association* (Fall): 74-86.

Courtenay, S. M., R. P. Crum, and S. B. Keller. 1989. Differential Reactions to Legislative Signaling during the Enactment of ERTA and TEFRA: An Empirical Investigation of Market Returns and Volume. *Journal of Accounting and Public Policy* (Winter): 283-321.

Cowell, F. A., and J. P. F. Gordon. 1988. Unwillingness to Pay: Tax Evasion and Public Good Provision. *Journal of Public Ecomonics* (August): 305-321.

Craig, D. L., and C. R. Enis. 1990. A Comparative Modeling of Tax Reform Before and After the Legislative Process. *Policy Sciences* (May): 133-161.

Cromwell, B. A. 1991. Public Sector Maintenance: The Case of Local Mass-Transit. *National Tax Journal* (June): 199-212.

Crum, R. P. 1985. Value-Added Tax Collection Alternatives: Their Revenue, Cash Flow, and Micro Tax Policy Effects. *Journal of the American Taxation Association* (Fall): 52-73.

——. 1991. Financing Value-Added Tax Cash Flows. *Journal of the American Taxation Association* (Spring): 1-35.

——, and B. H. Lubich. 1989. The Effect of Value-Added Tax Collection Alternatives on Revenue Yield, *Journal of the American Taxation Association* (Spring): 24-43.

Cutler, D. M. 1988. Tax Reform and the Stock Market: An Asset Price Approach. *American Economic Review* (December): 1107-1117.

Daly, M. J., J. Jung, P. Mercier, and T. Schweiter. 1987. The Taxation of Income from Capital in Canada: An International Comparison. *Canadian Tax Journal* (January-February): 88-119.

Davidson, S., and R. L. Weil. 1975. Inflation Accounting: What Will General Price Level Adjusted Income Statements Show? *Financial Analysts Journal* (January-February): 27-31, 71-84.

Downs, T., and P. H. Hendershott. 1987. Tax Policy and Stock Prices. *National Tax Journal* (June): 183-190.

———, and H. Tehranian. 1988. Predicting Stock Price Responses to Tax Policy Changes. *American Economic Review* (December): 1118-1129.

Dubin, J., and S. Henson. 1988. The Distributional Effects of the Federal Energy Tax Act. *Resources and Energy* (September): 191-212.

Douglas, A. V. 1990. Changes in Corporate Tax Revenue. *Canadian Tax Journal* (January/February): 66-81.

Dunbar, A., and S. Nordhauser. 1991. Is the Child Care Credit Progressive? *National Tax Journal* (December): 519-528.

Dworin, L., and E. B. Deakin. 1983. The Profitability of Outer Continental Shelf Drilling Ventures: An Alternative Approach. *National Tax Journal* (March): 57-64.

Eisner, R., S. H. Albert, and M. A. Sullivan. 1984. The New Incremental Tax Credit for R&D: Incentive or Disincentive. *National Tax Journal* (June): 171-183.

Enis, C. R., and D. L. Craig. 1984. The Redistribution of the Income Tax Burden under a True Flat Tax Structure. *Journal of the American Taxation Association* (Fall): 20-35.

——— and ———. 1990. An Empirical Analysis of Equity and Efficiency Attributes of Degressive Forms of a Flat Tax. *Journal of the American Taxation Association* (Spring): 17-33.

Feenberg, D., and J. Skinner. 1989. Sources of IRA Saving. In Lawerence Summers ed. *Tax Policy and the Economy* (National Bureau of Economic Research and MIT Press).

Feinstein, J. 1991. An Econometric Analysis of Income Tax Evasion and Its Detection. *Rand Journal of Economics* (Spring): 14-35.

Feldstein M. 1980. Inflation, Tax Rules and the Prices of Land and Gold. *Journal of Pulic Economics* (December): 309-317.

———. 1988. Imputing Corporate Tax Liabilities to Individual Taxpayers. *National Tax Journal* (March): 37-59.

Fellingham J. C., amd M. A. Wolfson. 1985. Taxes and Risk Sharing. *The Accounting Review* (January): 10-17.

———, and R. A. Young. 1989. Special Allocations, Investment Decisions, and Transaction Costs in Partnerships. *Journal of Accounting Research* (Autumn): 179-200.

Ferris, J. M. 1988. The Public Spending and Employment Effects of Local Service Contracting. *National Tax Journal* (June): 209-217.

Follain, J. R., and D. C. Ling. 1991. The Federal Tax Subsidy to Housing and the Reduced Value of the Mortgage Interest Deduction. *National Tax Journal* (June): 147-168.

Francis, J., and S. A. Reiter. 1987. Determinants of Corporate Pension Funding Strategy. *Journal of Accounting and Economics* (April): 35-60.

Friedman, B. F. 1982. Pension Funding, Pension Asset Allocation, and Corporate Finance: Evidence from Individual Company Data. Working Paper No. 957. (National Bureau of Economic Research).

Fuji, E. T., and C. B. Hawley. 1988. On the Accuracy of Tax Perceptions. *Review of Economics and Statistics* (May): 344-347.

Glenday, G., A. K. Gupta, and H. Pawlik. 1986. Tax Incentives for Personal Charitable Contributions. *Review of Economics and Statistics* (November): 688-693.

Grady, P. 1990a. The Distributional Impact of the Federal Tax and Transfer Changes Introduced Since 1984. *Canadian Tax Journal* (March-April): 286-297.

——. 1990b. An Analysis of the Distributional Impact of the Goods and Services Tax. *Canadian Tax Journal* (May-June): 632-643.

Guenther, D. A. 1992. Taxes and Organizational Form: A Comparison of Corporations and Master Limited Partnerships. *The Accounting Review* (January): 17-45.

Halperin, R. M., and W. N. Lanen. 1987. The Effects of Thor Power Tool Decision on the LIFO/FIFO Choice. *The Accounting Review* (April): 378-384.

——, and A. Maindiratta. 1989. On the Link Between Taxes and Incentives in the Choice of Business Form: The Case of Partnerships. *Journal of Accounting, Auditing & Finance* (Summer): 345-366.

——, and B. Srinidhi. 1987. The Effects of the U.S. Income Tax Regulations' Transfer Pricing Rules on Allocative Efficiency. *The Accounting Review* (October): 686-706.

——, and J. Tzur. 1985. The Effect of Nontaxable Employee Benefits on Employer Profits and Employee Work Effort. *National Tax Journal* (March): 65-79.

Hendershott, P. H., E. Toder, and Y. Won. 1991. Effects of Capital Gains Taxes on Revenue and Economic Efficiency. *National Tax Journal* (March): 21-37.

Hewitt, D. 1986. Fiscal Illusion from Grants and the Level of State and Federal Expenditures. *National Tax Journal* (December): 471-483.

Hirsch, W. Z., and A. M. Rufolo. 1986. Effects of State Income Taxes on Fringe Benefit Demand of Policemen and Firemen. *National Tax Journal* (June): 211-217.

Hite, G. L.. and M. S. Long. 1982. Taxes and Executive Stock Options. *Journal of Accounting and Economics* (July): 3-14.

Hite, P. A., and M. L. Roberts. 1991. An Experimental Investigation of Taxpayer Judgments on Rate Structure in the Individual Income Tax System. *Journal of the American Taxation Association* (Fall): 47-63.

Howard, R., G. Ruggeri, and D. Van Wart. 1991. The Progressivity of Provincial Personal Income Taxes in Canada. *Canadian Tax Journal* (No. 2): 288-308.

Hreha, K., and P. Silhan. 1986. An Empirical Analysis of Unitary Apportionment. *Journal of the American Taxation Association* (Fall): 7-18.

Hubbard, R. G. 1985. Personal Taxation, Pension Wealth, and Portfolio Composition. *Review of Economics and Statistics* (February): 53-60.

Internal Revenue Service. 1985. *Conference on Tax Administration Research—Proceedings.* (IRS, Office of the Assistant Commissioner).

——. 1987. *Survey of Tax Practitioners and Advisors: Summary of Results by Occupation.* Office of the Assistant Commissioner (Planning, Finance and Research).

——. 1988. *The Role of Tax Practitioners in the Tax System* (March).

Jackson. B., and V. Milliron. 1989. Tax Preparers: Government Agents or Client Advocates? *Journal of Accountancy* (May): 76-82.

——, ——, and D. R. Toy. 1988. Tax Practitioners and the Government. *Tax Notes* (October 17): 333-341.

Joulfaian, D. 1991. Charitable Bequests and Estate Taxes. *National Tax Journal* (June): 169-180.

Kachelmeier, S. J., S. T. Limberg, and M. S. Schadewald. 1991. A Laboratory Market Examination of the Consumer Price Response to Information about Producers' Costs. *The Accounting Review* (October): 694-717.

Kau, J. B., and D. Keenan. 1983. Inflation, Taxes and Housing: A Theoretical Analysis. *Journal of Public Economics* (June): 93-104.

King, R., and D. Wallin. 1990. Individual Risk-Taking and Income Taxes: An Experimental Examination. *Journal of The American Taxation Association* (Fall): 26-38.

Kitchen, H., and R. Dalton. 1990. Determinants of Charitable Donations by Families in Canada: A Regional Analysis. *Applied Economics* (March): 285-299.

Kolm, S-C. 1973. A Note on Optimal Tax Evasion. *Journal of Public Economics* (July): 265-270.

Kramer, S. S. 1982. Blockage: Valuation of Large Blocks of Publicly Traded Stocks for Tax Purposes. *The Accounting Review* (January): 70-87.

Ladd, H. F., and K. L. Bradbury. 1988. City Taxes and Property Tax Bases. *National Tax Journal* (December): 503-523.

Lewellen, W., C. Loderer, and K. Martin. 1987. Executive Compensation and Executive Incentive Problems: An Empirical Analysis. *Journal of Accounting and Economics* (December): 287-310.

Long, J. E. 1988. Taxation and IRA Participation: Re-Examination and Confirmation. *National Tax Journal* (December): 585-589.

———, and S. B. Caudill. 1987. The Usage and Benefits of Paid Tax Return Preparation. *National Tax Journal* (March): 35-46.

———, and J. D. Gwartney. 1987. Income Tax Avoidance: Evidence from Individual Tax Returns. *National Tax Journal* (December): 517-532.

Lowenstein, M. A., and J. E. McLure. 1988. Taxes and Financial Leasing. *Quarterly Review of Economics and Business* (Spring): 21-38.

Lyon, A. 1989. The Effect of the Investment Tax Credit on the Value of the Firm. *Journal of Public Economics* (March): 227-247.

Luttman, S. M. 1990. Enriching Tax Research Through Database Merging. *Journal of the American Taxation Association* (Spring): 69-75.

Macnaughton, A. 1992. Fringe Benefits and Employee Expenses: Tax Planning and Neutral Tax Policy. *Contemporary Accounting Research* (Fall).

Madeo, L. A., and S. A. Madeo. 1984. The Equity and Motivating Effects of the Maximum Tax. *Journal of the American Taxation Association* (Spring): 40-49.

Madeo S., and M. Pinches. 1985. Stock Market Behavior and Tax Rule Changes: The Case of the Disallowance of Certain Interest Deductions Claimed by Banks. *The Accounting Review* (July): 407-429.

———, A. Schepanski, and W. C. Uecker. 1987. Modeling Judgments of Taxpayer Compliance. *The Accounting Review* (April): 323-342.

Maslove, A. M. 1989. *Tax Reform in Canada: The Process and Impact* (Ottawa: Institute for Research on Public Policy).

Marchant, G., J. Robinson, U. Anderson, and M. Schadewald. 1991. Analogical Transfer and Expertise in Legal Reasoning. *Organizational Behavior and Human Decision Processes* (April): 272-290.

McCarty, T. A. 1990. The Effect of Social Security on Married Women's Labor Force Participation. *National Tax Journal* (March): 95-110.

Mead, W. J., D. D. Muraoka, and P. E. Sorensen. 1982. The Effect of Taxes on the Profitability of U.S. Oil and Gas Production: A Case Study of the OCS Record. *National Tax Journal* (March): 21-29.

Meade, J. 1990. The Impact of Different Capital Gains Tax Regimes on the Lock in Effect and New Risky Investment Decisions. *The Accounting Review* (April): 406-431.

Meng, R., and W. I. Gillespie. 1986. Horizontal Equity and Property Taxation in Canada. *National Tax Journal* (June): 221-227.

Metcalf, G. E. 1991. The Role of Federal Taxation in the Supply of Municipal Bonds: Evidence from Municipal Governments. *National Tax Journal* (December): 57-79.

Mieszkowski, P. 1969. Tax Incidence Theory: The Effects of Taxes on the Distribution of Income. *Journal of Economic Literature* (December): 1103-1124.

Milliron, V. C. 1985. A Behavioral Study of the Meaning and Influence of Tax Complexity. *Journal of Accounting Research* (Autumn): 794-816.

Mittelstaedt, H. F. 1989. An Empirical Analysis of the Factors Underlying the Decision to Remove Excess Assets from Overfunded Pension Plans. *Journal of Accounting and Economics* (November): 399-418.

Morgan, W. E., and J. H. Mutti. 1985. The Explortation of State and Local Taxes in a Multilateral Framework: The Case of Business Type Taxes. *National Tax Journal* (June): 191-208.

Morrison, R. J., and J. Oderkirk. 1991. Married and Umarried Couples: The Tax Question. *Canadian Social Trends* (Summer): 15-20.

Mumy, G. E. 1985. The Role of Taxes and Social Security in Determining the Structure of Wages and Pensions. *Journal of Political Economy* (June): 574-585.

Murphy, B., and M. C. Wolfson. 1991. When the Baby Boom Grows Old: Impacts on Canada's Public Sector. *The Statistical Journal of the United Nations Economic Commission for Europe* (vol. 8, no. 1): 25-44.

Omer, T. C., K. H. Molloy, and D. Ziebart. 1991. Measurement of Effective Corporate Tax Rates Using Financial Statement Information. *Journal of the American Taxation Association* (Spring): 57-72.

———, and W. H. Shaw. 1991. Methodological Problems in Empirical Market-Based Tax Research. In *A Guide to Tax Research Methodologies*, C. R. Enis, ed. (American Accounting Association): 28-41.

———, and S. A. Reiter. 1991. Measuring Tax Incentives. Working Paper. (University of Illinois).

O'Neil, C. J., D. V. Saftner, and M. P. Dillaway. 1983. Premature Withdrawals from Individual Retirement Accounts: A Breakeven Analysis. *Journal of the American Taxation Association* (Spring): 35-43.

———, and G. R. Thompson. 1987. Participation in Individual Retirement Accounts: An Empirical Investigation. *National Tax Journal* (December): 617-624.

——— and ———. 1988. Taxation and IRA Participation: A Response to Long. *National Tax Journal* (December): 591-593.

———, J. M. Cathey, and T. K. Flesher. 1988. An Analysis of Ph.D. Dissertations in Taxation: 1977-1985. *Issues in Accounting Education* (Spring): 120-130.

Outslay, E., and J. E. Wheeler. 1982. Separating the Annuity and Income Transfer Elements of Social Security. *The Accounting Review* (October): 716-733.

Papke, L. E. 1987. Subnational Taxation and Capital Mobility: Estimates of Tax Price Elasticities. *National Tax Journal* (June): 191-203.

Pasurka, C. A. 1984. Corporate Income Taxes and U.S. Effective Rates of Protection. *National Tax Journal* (December): 529-537.

Pechman, J. A., and G. V. Engelhardt. 1990. The Income Tax Treatment of the Family: An International Perspective. *National Tax Journal* (March): 1-22.

Pierce, B. J. 1989. Homeowner Preferences: The Equity and Revenue Effects of Proposed Changes in the Status Quo. *Journal of the American Taxation Association* (Spring): 54-67.

Pitt, M. M., and J. Slemrod. 1989. The Compliance Cost of Itemizing Deductions: Evidence from Individual Tax Returns. *American Economic Review* (December): 1224-1232.

Pollard, W. B., and R. M. Copeland. 1985. Evaluating the Robustness of Multivariate Tax Models to Errors: A Section 162(a)(2) Illustration. *Journal of the American Taxation Association* (Fall): 7-18.

Porcano, T. M. 1986. Corprate Tax Rates: Progressive, Proportional, or Regressive. *Journal of the American Taxation Association* (Spring): 17-31.

———. 1987. Government Tax Incentives and Fixed Asset Acquisitions: A Comparative Study of Four Industrial Countries. *Journal of the American Taxation Association* (Fall): 7-23.

Preston, A. E., and C. Ichniowski. 1991. A National Perspective on the Nature and Effects of the Local Property Tax Revolt, 1976-1986. *National Tax Journal* (June): 123-145.

Quigley, J. M., and D. L. Rubinfeld. 1991. Private Guarantees for Municipal Bonds: Evidence from the Aftermarket. *National Tax Journal* (December): 29-39.

Reckers, P. M., D. L. Sanders, and R. W. Wyndelts. 1991. An Empirical Investigation of Factors Influencing Tax Practitioner Compliance. *Journal of the American Taxation Association* (Fall): 30-46.

Reece, W. 1979. Charitable Contributions: New Evidence on Household Behavior. *American Economic Review* (March): 142-151.

Reinganum, J. F., and L. L. Wilde. 1985. Income Tax Compliance in a Principal-Agent Framework. *Journal of Public Economics* (February): 1-18.

Ricketts, R. C. 1990. Social Security Growth Versus Income Tax Reform: An Analysis of Progressivity and Horizontal Equity in the Federal Tax System in the 1980s. *Journal of the American Taxation Association* (Spring): 34-50.

Ricks, W. 1982. The Markets Response to the 1974 LIFO Adoptions. *Journal of Accounting Research* (Autumn): 367-387.

Robinson, J. R. 1990. Estimates of the Price Elasticity of Charitable Giving: A Reappraisal Using 1985 Itemizer and Nonitemizer Charitable Deduction Data. *Journal of the American Taxation Association* (Fall): 35-59.

Rock, S. M. 1984. The Impact of Deductibility on the Incidence of a General Sales Tax. *National Tax Journal* (March): 105-112.

Schepanski, A., and D. Kelsey. 1990. Testing for Framing Effects in Taxpayer Compliance Decisions. *Journal of the American Taxation Association* (Fall): 60-77.

Schiff, J. 1985. Does Government Spending Crowd Out Charitable Contributions. *National Tax Journal* (December): 535-545.

Schipper, K., and R. Thompson. 1983. The Impact of Merger-Related Regulations on the Shareholders of Acquiring Firms. *Journal of Accounting Research* (Spring): 184-221.

————, ————, and R. Weil. 1987. Disentangling Interrelated Effects of Regulatory Changes on Shareholder Wealth: The Case of Motor Carrier Deregulation. *Journal of Law and Economics* (April): 67-100.

Schmidt, D. R. 1986. Apportionment of Multijurisdictional Corporate Income. *Journal of the American Taxation Association* (Fall): 19-34.

Scholes, M. S., G. P. Wilson, and M. A. Wolfson. 1990. Tax Planning, Regulatory Capital Planning, and Financial Reporting Strategy for Commercial Banks. *Review of Financial Studies*: 625-650.

————, and M. A. Wolfson. 1992. *Taxes and Business Strategy: A Planning Approach.* Prentice-Hall.

Shaw W. 1988. Measuring the Impact of the Safe Harbor Lease Law on Security Prices. *Journal of Accounting Research* (Spring): 60-81.

Shevlin, T. 1987. Taxes and Off-Balance-Sheet Financing: Research and Development Limited Partnerships. *The Accounting Review* (July): 480-509.

————. 1990. Estimating Corporate Marginal Tax Rates with Asymmetric Tax Treatment of Gains and Losses. *Journal of the American Taxation Association* (Spring): 51-67.

————. 1991. The Valuation of R&D Firms with R&D Limited Partnerships. *The Accounting Review* (January): 1-21.

————. and S. Porter. 1992. The Corporate Tax Comeback in 1987: Some Further Evidence. *Journal of the American Taxation Association* (Spring): 58-79.

Slemrod, J. 1982. The Effect of Capital Gains Taxation on Year-End Stock Market Behavior. *National Tax Journal* (March): 69-77.

————. 1985. An Empirical Test for Tax Evasion. *Review of Economics and Statistics* (May): 232-238.

————. 1989. Are Estimated Tax Elasticities Really Just Tax Evasion Elasticities? The Case of Charitable Contributions. *Review of Economics and Statistics* (August): 517-522.

————, and N. Sorum. 1984. The Compliance Cost of the U.S. Individual Tax System. *National Tax Journal* (December): 461-474.

————, and S. Yitzhaki. 1983. On Choosing a Flat-Rate Income Tax System. *National Tax Journal* (March): 31-44.

Srinivasan, T. N. 1973. Tax Evasion: A Model. *Journal of Public Economics* (November): 339-346.

Stickney, C. P., and V. E. McGee. 1982. Effective Corporate Tax Rates: The Effect of Size, Capital Intensity, Leverage, and Other Factors. *Journal of Accounting and Public Policy* (Winter): 125-152.

Stockfisch, J. A. 1985. Value-Added Taxes and the Size of Government: Some Evidence. *National Tax Journal* (December): 547-552.

Swenson, C. W. 1987. An Analysis of ACRS During Inflationary Periods. *The Accounting Review* (January): 117-136.

———. 1988. Taxpayer Behavior in Response to Taxation: An Experimental Analysis. *Journal of Accounting and Public Policy* (Spring): 1-28.

———. 1989. Tax Regimes and the Demand for Risky Assets: Some Experimental Market Evidence. *Journal of the American Taxation Association* (Fall): 54-76.

Tanzi, V. 1987. The Responses of Other Industrial Countries to the U.S. Tax Reform Act. *National Tax Journal* (September): 339-355.

Thomas, J. K. 1988. Corporate Taxes and Defined Benefit Pension Plans. *Journal of Accounting and Economics* (July): 199-237.

———. 1989. Why Do Firms Terminate Their Overfunded Pension Plans. *Journal of Accounting and Economics* (November): 361-398.

Thornton, D. B. 1987. Inflation, Accounting and the Canadian Corporate Tax Base. *Canadian Journal of Administrative Sciences* (March): 66-96.

Van Wart, D., and G. Ruggeri. 1990. The Effects of Tax Reform on the Elasticity of the Personal Income Tax. *Canadian Tax Journal* (September-October): 1210-1226.

Venti, S. F., and D. A. Wise. 1988. The Determinants of IRA Contributions and the Effects of Limit Changes. In Z. Bodie, J. Shoven and D. Wise (eds.) *Pensions in the U.S. Economy* (University of Chicago Press and National Bureau of Economic Research, 1988).

Verrecchia, R. E. 1982. An Analysis of Two Cost Allocation Cases. *The Accounting Review* (July): 579-593.

Wallace, S., M. Wasylenko, and D. Weiner. 1991. The Distributional Implications of the 1986 Tax Reform. *National Tax Journal* (June): 181-198.

Watson, H. 1988, The Effects of Taxation on Partnership Investment. *Journal of Public Economics* (June): 111-126.

Weiss, R. D. 1979. Effective Corporation Income Tax Rates. *National Tax Journal* (September): 380-389.

Wheaton, W. C. 1983. Interstate Differences in the Level of Business Taxation. *National Tax Journal* (March): 83-94.

Whittington, R., and G. Whittenburg. 1980. Judicial Classification of Debt Versus Equity— An Empirical Study. *The Accounting Review* (July): 409-418.

Wilkie, P. J. 1988. Corporate Average Effective Tax Rates and Inferences About Relative Tax Preference. *Journal of the American Taxation Association* (Fall): 75-88.

———, and S. T. Limberg. 1990. The Relationship Between Firm Size and Effective Tax Rate: A Reconciliation of Zimmerman [1983] and Porcano [1986]. *Journal of the American Taxation Association* (Spring): 76-91.

Wilson, G. P. 1991. Future Research Directions in Taxation. *Journal of the American Taxation Association* (Fall): 64-73.

Wiseman, M. 1989. Proposition 13 and Effective Property Tax Rates. *Public Finance Quarterly* (October): 391-408.

Wolfson, M. A. 1985. Tax, Incentive, and Risk-Sharing Issues in the Allocation of Property Rights: The Generalized Lease-or-Buy Problem. *Journal of Business* (April): 159-171.

Yankelovich, Skelly, and White, Inc. 1984. *Taxpayer Attitudes Study Final Report.* (Internal Revenue Service).

Young, K. H. 1988. The Effects of Taxes and Rates of Return on Foreign Direct Investment in the United States. *National Tax Journal* (March): 109-121.

Zimmerman, J. L. 1983. Taxes and Firm Size. *Journal of Accounting and Economics* (August): 119-149.

Chapter 2
Data on Tax Compliance

Robert C. Ricketts
Texas Tech University

Introduction

Researchers at the Internal Revenue Service have gathered information on compliance levels, the income and tax characteristics of compliers and noncompliers, and the attitudes of those individuals (taxpayers and tax preparers) most closely involved in the tax filing process. Much of this data is available to academic researchers outside the IRS who are interested in tax compliance research.

This chapter discusses three data bases accumulated by the IRS which are available to researchers: the *Taxpayer Compliance Measurement Program (TCMP)* file, the *Survey of Taxpayer Opinions* file, and the *Survey of Tax Practitioners and Advisers* file. The discussion focuses on the purpose behind the studies which produced each data base, the sampling procedures used in generating the files, the nature and quality of the data provided in each file, and the necessary procedures for obtaining access to each file.

SECTION 1: TCMP DATA

The Taxpayer Compliance Measurement Program (TCMP) is used by the IRS to statistically distinguish compliers and noncompliers for the primary purpose of more accurately identifying potential noncompliers. The program involves a series of exhaustive audits conducted periodically on a stratified random sample of taxpayers.

The TCMP program encompasses all types of tax returns. The most common, the individual tax return program, has been repeated every three years since 1973.[1] TCMP audits have also been performed on small-to-medium corporations (1969, 1973, 1978, 1981, and 1988), estate returns (1971), exempt organization returns (1974, 1979, and 1986), fiduciary returns (1975), employee plans returns (1980), partnership returns (1982), and S corporation returns (1985). Because data are currently available from the IRS only for the 1979, 1982, 1985, and 1988 Individual Income Tax Return Surveys, and the 1981 and 1987 Corporate Return Surveys, the following discussion will be limited to those files. Readers should refer to *The TCMP Handbook* (IRS, 1989) for a more thorough discussion of the TCMP Files, especially the nonindividual/noncorporate files.[2]

---

[1] Prior to 1973, audits were conducted in 1963, 1965, and 1969.

[2] For previous published studies using TCMP data, see Clotfelter (1983), Madeo, Schepanksi, and Uecker (1987), Dubin and Henson (1988), Slemrod (1989), Chang and Schultz (1990), and Feinstein (1991). For discussions of trends identified using TCMP data, see IRS (1986), and Wilt and Perng (1988).

Special thanks to Doug Shackelford, Charles Christian, and Sue Long for their helpful comments and assistance in this project.

Overview of the TCMP Data Base

Purpose of the Program. The TCMP Program serves two essential purposes. First, TCMP data provide an important source of information for estimating the size of the "tax gap" for voluntary filers of individual and corporate tax returns. The TCMP data measure the difference between taxes reported and taxes owed, as determined by the IRS, for a randomly selected sample of taxpayers. This information can then be extrapolated to the entire population of taxpayers using the sample weights associated with each stratum of the random sample.

The second, and more important, purpose of the TCMP program is to provide unbiased statistical information to be used in the development of the discriminant function (DIF) used to distinguish between compliers and noncompliers. This DIF function is then used in future years to select returns for potential audit.

Sampling Procedure. The Individual TCMP files average around 50,000 observations (taxpayers), while the Corporate files contain 33,000 observations. In both cases, the samples are stratified random samples chosen using the Taxpayer Identification Numbers provided on the returns (social security numbers for individuals; employer identification numbers for corporations). As in the Statistics of Income data files, stratification is based on a variety of return characteristics (income level, source(s) of income, etc.). However, in the TCMP stratification process, two additional criteria must be met. First, each sample stratum must reliably represent the associated segment of the overall population of returns. Second, each stratum must contain at least 500 "profitable to audit" tax returns in each class (IRS, 1989, 10). Returns are profitable to audit if the resulting change in tax liability and penalties exceeds pre-determined amounts. Using these criteria, the samples are stratified into 10 different audit classes (eight for corporations) as indicated in Table 1.

Data Available. The TCMP files provide an extremely rich source of data for tax compliance research. Most significant, the TCMP files allow computation of a direct measure of voluntary compliance, both in the aggregate and with regard to specific items. An aggregate measure of compliance commonly used in TCMP research, voluntary compliance level (VCL), is computed from information provided in the file as the ratio of reported tax liability to reported tax liability plus identified tax deficiencies, exclusive of penalties:

$$VCL = \frac{\text{Tax Reported}}{\text{Reported Liability + Identified Deficiencies}} \times 100\%$$

Alternatively, researchers can compute similar measures specific to certain categories of income, loss, deduction, or credit. Because the TCMP files provide both reported and corrected information from sample tax returns, researchers can compute similar compliance levels for capital gain income, income from sources not subject to information reporting, etc.

As summarized in Tables 2 and 3, the TCMP files contain specific information about a variety of items for each sample tax return. For individuals, information provided can be classified into five categories (Table 2). The first category contains

TABLE 1
Audit Classes Identified in the TCMP Files

Panel A: Individual Income Tax Returns

Class	Description
1	Nonbusiness Income with TPI[1] < $25,000, 1040A
2	Nonbusiness Income with TPI < $25,000, non-1040A
3	Nonbusiness Income with $25,000 < TPI < $50,000
4	Nonbusiness Income with $50,000 < TPI < $100,000
5	Nonbusiness Income with TPI > $100,000
6	Self-Employed: TGR[2] < $25,000, Schedule C
7	Self-Employed: $25,000 < TGR < $100,000, Sch C
8	Self-Employed: TGR > $100,000, Schedule C
9	Self-Employed: TGR < $100,000, Schedule F
10	Self-Employed: TGR > $100,000, Schedule F

Panel B: Corporate Tax Returns

Class	Description
1	Total Assets < $50,000
2	$50,000 < Total Assets < $100,000
3	$100,000 < Total Assets < $250,000
4	$250,000 < Total Assets < $500,000
5	$500,000 < Total Assets < $1,000,000
6	$1,000,000 < Total Assets < $5,000,000
7	$5,000,000 < Total Assets < $10,000,000
8	No balance sheet corporations

[1] Total Positive Income = sum of all positive nonbusiness income amounts.
[2] Total Gross Receipts = sum of all receipts on Schedules C and F.

information about the TCMP examiner, including the G.S. level, and the time spent on the examination. These variables might be used to control for differences in experience among the examiners, or perhaps as indicators of return complexity. The second category of information consists of information regarding the preparer of the return, primarily whether the return was self-prepared or professionally prepared, and if the latter, the professional status (CPA, attorney, etc.) of the preparer.

The third category of information provided in the Individual TCMP files contains data on the demographic characteristics of the taxpayer being examined. Variables in this category include the taxpayer's occupation, audit class, filing status, ZIP code, and number and type of dependents. In addition, a disposition code indicates whether the taxpayer agreed or disagreed with the examiner's adjustments, and whether an appeal was filed.

The bulk of the information provided in the Individual TCMP file falls into category four, tax return information. Both reported and "corrected" amounts[3] are

[3] Examiner corrections may be inaccurate as well. The taxpayer agreement variable, and information on whether the taxpayer chose to appeal or not to appeal the examiner's findings (also provided on the TCMP tape) may shed some additional light on this question.

TABLE 2
Data Provided in Individual TCMP Files

Category	Relevant Variables	
IRS Examiner		Time Spent on Examination
		G.S. Code
		District Office
Tax Preparer		Type of Preparer (CPA, etc.)
		Taxpayer Service Used?
Taxpayer Information	Demographics	Occupation (82 and 85 only)
		Filing Status
		Number/Type of Dependents
		Audit Class
		ZIP Code
		Agreement with Examiner Adj?
Tax Return Information	Form 1040	Reported & Corrected Amounts for all line items on 1040, including Schedules A and B
	Capital Gains	Sales Price and Gain/Loss for short and long-term assets
	Schedules C/F	Reported & Corrected Amounts for each line item
		Principal Industrial Activity Code for Schedule C
	Passive Activities	Reported & Corrected Amounts
		Reason(s) for Correction
	Penalties	Type & Amount of Penalties assessed by examiner
Nature of Noncompliance	General	Prior or Subsequent Yr adj?
		Foreign Entity Transactions?
		Material Participation?
		Capital Gain Dist?
		Amended Return?
		Principal Reason for Adjustment? (substantiation, uncertainty, error, etc.)
	Filing Requirements	Required 1099s Filed?
		5500 Filed if Necessary?
		Nature of Retirement Plans?

provided for each line item on the Form 1040 and Schedules A and B. In addition, complete information is provided for reported and corrected amounts on Schedules C and F, and summary information is provided for amounts on Schedule E. Some additional information is provided on capital gains and passive activity losses, and a summary of the types and amounts of penalties assessed is available.

The final category of information provided in the Individual TCMP file concerns the nature of the noncompliance *detected by the examiner*. As noted previously, the taxpayer's overall compliance level can be measured by reference to the total tax deficiencies identified by the TCMP examiner. Similar measures can be computed for specific categories of income or loss using the specific tax return information provided. But the TCMP file also contains other noncompliance information related to the *nature* of detected noncompliance. Did the taxpayer file all necessary payor information returns? Were adjustments required for previous or subsequent year returns? Were any adjustments due to improper reporting of capital gains distributions, or to the taxpayer's failure to materially participate in a loss activity? Was the return amended prior to examination? Was any part of the adjustment due to a transaction involving a foreign entity? Finally, the file provides an indication of the *primary* reason for the examiner's *net* adjustment to the taxpayer's tax liability. This variable is categorical, indicating whether the primary factor was a lack of substantiation, a dispute over the proper application of the tax law, a computational error, a preparer error, taxpayer ignorance, or some other reason. This variable may help to differentiate between intentional and unintentional noncompliance.

As summarized in Table 3, similar information is provided in the Corporate TCMP file. The primary differences in the two files are related to the differences in the types of taxpayers examined. Thus, the "taxpayer" data in the corporate file provides information about the size (total assets) and age of the sample entity, as well as its principal business activity. Tax return information is similarly comprehensive, although it is important to note that no balance sheet information (other than total assets) is provided. Finally, less information is provided regarding the nature of detected noncompliance, although some information is available regarding whether corporate officers or shareholders were involved in the noncompliance, or whether improper reporting behavior was confined to the corporate return.

Data Limitations

Though perhaps the richest source of data for tax compliance research, there are limitations to the TCMP data. First, TCMP provides information only on *detected noncompliance*. Unreported income is often difficult to detect and some such income surely goes unnoticed by examiners, so that noncompliance levels may be understated for some taxpayers. Second, adjustments to income, deductions, or tax liability reported in the TCMP files are those determined necessary by the examiners; in cases where the proper interpretation of the law is unclear, these adjustments may overstate noncompliance levels. Finally, the Service notes that the TCMP sample is designed to provide national estimates of the level of noncompliance and may not be large enough to provide reliable estimates at the regional or district level (IRS 1989, 6).

Data Access

Direct access to the TCMP files is limited to research projects which, in the opinion of the Service, make the greatest contributions to the IRS or the research community. Moreover, due to the highly confidential nature of the data involved, the data will not be released to parties outside the Service. Thus, studies by academic researchers must be done in partnership with the Service.[4]

---

[4] A wealth of aggregated TCMP data, and some microlevel data from early surveys, are available from the Transactional Records Access Clearinghouse at Syracuse University. The Clearinghouse provides

(Continued on next page)

TABLE 3
Data Provided in Corporate TCMP Files

Category	Relevant Variables	
IRS Examiner		Time Spent on Examination
		G.S. Code
		District Office
Entity		Form 1120 or 1120A?
		Date of Incorporation?
		Business Code
		Total Assets
		Consolidated Return?
		Initial/Final Return?
		Closely held?
		Type of Preparer?
Return Information	Income	Reported & Corrected for lines 1-11, Form 1120
	Deductions	Reported & Corrected for lines 12-29, Form 1120
	Tax Comp	Reported & Corrected taxes, credits and payments
	Additional Info.	Reported and Corrected answers to "Additional Information" questions on p. 3 of 1120
	Depreciation	Reported & Corrected, total and Schedule A
	Penalties	Nature & Amount of penalties assessed by examiner
Nature of Noncompliance	Payor Info. Returns	1098/1099s filed? Currency Transaction Reports filed?
	Payee Info. Returns	Reported and Corrected amounts from 1099s
	International Transactions	Adj. due to International transactions?
	Misclassified	Adj. arising from misclassification?
	Real Estate Sales	Reported and Unreported sales of real estate
	Officers/ Shareholders	Returns filed? Related examinations required?

Footnote 4 (Continued from previous page)

   SAS data sets, on magnetic tape, containing information aggregated by line item and audit class, type of adjustment and audit class, and net tax misreporting by line on the TCMP checksheet. Aggregated panel data are also available tracking noncompliance by year, region and audit class, and by line item on the return, year and audit class. The most recent data currently available are from the 1985 TCMP. For additional information regarding this data, as well as data sets on audits, criminal prosecutions, IRS Personnel and other IRS activities, contact Susan B. Long, Transactional Records Access Clearinghouse, 478 Newhouse II, Syracuse University, Syracuse, N.Y. 13244 (315-443-3563).

Researchers granted access to the files must write the computer programs necessary to analyze the data. These programs will then be run by the IRS internally and results will be made available to the researcher(s) for analysis. As noted above, no actual data will be released by the Service. In this regard, researchers will need to be fairly computer literate; not only will the programming phase of the research project be "hands off" relative to analyses where the researcher has direct access to the data, but the files are stored in binary format rather than the standard SAS or SPSS format common to many other data sources used in tax research (such as the Ernst & Young/University of Michigan Panel Tapes). The files can be analyzed, however, using SAS, SPSS or FORTRAN programming languages.

To obtain access to the TCMP files, interested researchers must submit a research proposal summarizing the research question, the theoretical framework within which the question will be addressed, the research method to be used, and a projected timetable for completion of the project. The proposal is not to exceed 10 pages and should be submitted, along with the vita(e) of the researcher(s), to the IRS at the following address:

> Research Division PFR:R
> Attention: Compliance Research Coordinator
> Internal Revenue Service
> 1111 Constitution Avenue, NW
> Washington, DC 20024

Proposals are considered annually, and generally must be submitted by March 30 to be considered. Evaluation of the proposals takes place in three stages. First, proposals are screened to insure that they do not compromise the security of the DIF function. Second, the proposals are evaluated internally by Service personnel using the criteria of interest to the Service and research community, and reasonableness with regard to IRS resource requirements. The third stage then involves evaluation by a panel of outside researchers interested in tax compliance research. For more information on the proposal process, contact the IRS at the above address and request an *Informational Packet for TCMP Research Proposals*.

SECTION 2: THE 1987 TAXPAYER OPINION SURVEY

Although the TCMP files provide detailed information on the financial and tax characteristics of compliers and noncompliers, they provide relatively little information on taxpayer demographics and no information on taxpayer attitudes. In an effort to investigate the effects of these factors on noncompliance behavior, the Service commissioned a survey of taxpayer attitudes in 1987.[5] The 1987 *Taxpayer*

---

[5] The 1987 survey was actually the fourth national survey of taxpayer attitudes. The first survey was completed in 1968 and measured a variety of taxpayer opinions on compliance issues. The second and third surveys were completed in 1980 and 1984, and measured both taxpayer opinions and admitted noncompliance behavior. A fifth survey was conducted in 1990, the data from which have not yet been released by the Service. This data should be publicly available by 1993. Researchers interested in obtaining the 1984 Survey File or the 1990 Survey File (when it becomes available) should contact the IRS.

Opinion Survey requested information from a nationwide sample of taxpayers regarding their attitudes toward the IRS, and the tax system in general. The survey also asked sample taxpayers about their own compliance behavior. This data, together with the demographic information collected, may be useful in exploring for relationships between taxpayer attitudes and demographic characteristics and compliance behavior.[6]

Overview of the 1987 Taxpayer Opinion Survey

Purpose of the Survey. The 1987 *Taxpayer Opinion Survey* was designed to accomplish a variety of objectives. First, the study enables the Service to measure taxpayer attitudes potentially related to noncompliance behavior. Second, the IRS can determine which, if any, of these attitudes is most strongly related to admitted noncompliance behavior, and/or perceptions of the noncompliance behavior of others. Third, the Service can assess public support for certain types of noncompliance activities and for noncompliers in general. Finally, the Service sought feedback on taxpayer perceptions of its performance and recommendations for how it might improve its effectiveness.

Sampling Procedure. The survey sample was designed to provide statistically reliable estimates of taxpayer attitudes and compliance behavior at a national level. The sample is stratified twice — first, by geographic region, and second, by metropolitan and nonmetropolitan areas within each region. Regionally, the sample is comprised of four major geographic segments — Atlantic, Southern, Mid-Central, and Western. Locally, respondents are classified as residing in a central city area, within a Standard Metropolitan Statistical Area (SMSA) but outside the central city, or outside an SMSA. The resulting sample is thus stratified on 12 levels, as summarized in Table 4.

A total of 2,003 households were contacted across the 12 strata. Within each household, interviewers requested an interview with the person most familiar with filing a tax return.[7] Of the 2,003 households contacted, 1,756 primary filers were interviewed. The remaining 247 respondents were classified as nonfilers.

Information provided for nonfilers is dependent upon their reasons for not filing. For those who were not required to file due to age or retirement status, the survey collected information on their views of the 1986 tax reform and demographics only.[8] More complete survey information is available for other nonfilers, although no data was collected on questions related to evaluation of the IRS or personal compliance behavior since these issues are not relevant to individuals not filing returns.

---

[6] For more information about the survey, including the survey instrument and the surveyor's analysis of the responses, see Louis Harris & Associates (1987a). For a similar analysis of taxpayer attitudes from the 1984 Taxpayer Opinion Survey (also publicly available from the IRS), see IRS (1985) and Yankelovich, Skelly and White (1984). For an analysis of trends in taxpayers' opinions, based on these and other surveys, see Broehm and Sharp (1989), and Louis Harris & Associates (1987b).

[7] Where multiple adults resided in a household, and more than one was a primary filer, respondents were chosen randomly from the pool of qualified filers.

[8] The bulk of nonfilers claimed exemption from filing based on age or retirement status.

TABLE 4
Geographic Stratification of the 1987
Taxpayer Opinion Survey

Regional Strata	Local Strata
Atlantic	
	Central City
Southern	
	Rest of SMSA
Mid-Central	
	Outside SMSA
Western	

In summary, the 1987 Taxpayer Attitudes Survey provides detailed information regarding the attitudes and admitted behavior of a nationally representative sample of over 2,000 taxpayers and nonfilers. Because sample selection was designed to obtain a targeted number of completed interviews from each sample stratum, each region of the country should be represented proportionally.

Data Available. The survey provides responses to 121 questions asked of primary filers. Many questions contain multiple subparts, however, so that there are over 300 response variables for each taxpayer-respondent. For nonfilers, many questions were not relevant, but information is available on more than 150 response variables for nonfilers (other than the elderly and retired).

The data can be loosely classified into four general categories: (1) attitudes toward the tax system and society in general, (2) personal compliance behavior and perceptions of, and attitudes toward, the noncompliant behavior of others, (3) questions evaluating the effectiveness and quality of IRS services, and (4) demographic information. The following discussion summarizes the major issues addressed in the survey instrument.

Issues Addressed

Taxpayer Attitudes. As summarized in Table 5, the survey measured taxpayer attitudes in two areas. First, respondents were asked about their attitudes toward the income tax system in general. Since the survey was conducted in 1987, respondents were first asked for their opinions of the Tax Reform Act of 1986. Questions about tax reform focused on how well-informed respondents were about the specific changes imposed, and whether they perceived the Act to have enhanced or diminished overall levels of equity in the income tax system. Other questions probed more directly into general attitudes about, and perceptions of, the system. For example, respondents were asked whether they felt the income tax system to be generally fair, or whether, in their opinion, some taxpayers or groups of taxpayers (especially the wealthy) are able to take advantage of "loopholes" to unfairly reduce their relative burdens.[9] Other questions asked respondents what portion of tax

---

[9] Both horizontal and vertical dimensions of equity were addressed.

cheaters they think are actually caught by the IRS, and how severely those who are caught are likely to be punished.[10] Additionally, respondents were asked to evaluate, on a six-point scale, how complicated the tax laws are for them personally.

The second set of attitudes measured, referred to as "psychographics" in the survey instrument, reflect respondents' opinions about society in general. As indicated in Table 5, the survey measured five basic types of societal attitudes. Respondents were asked how much importance should be placed on obedience and respect for authority, and whether they believe that public officials are generally trustworthy. With regard to human integrity, the survey asked whether respondents believe that most people are basically trustworthy or whether honesty is related primarily to the fear of being caught. Disenfranchisement refers to the degree of control respondents feel they have over their own life: do most of the events in people's lives result from things over which they have no control? Finally, the survey measures respondents' agreement with the idea that people must take chances in order to get ahead.

Compliance Behavior and Perceptions. A substantial number of questions address compliance issues. In general, the survey addressed four aspects of taxpayer compliance. The first area of investigation concerns respondent sympathies for specific types of noncompliance behavior. Two attitudinal dimensions are explored here. First, respondents were asked questions concerning the acceptability of various illegal transactions (see Table 6). A second set of questions addressed respondents' sympathies for various rationales supporting noncompliance (Table 7). Thus, respondents were asked first whether they found certain specific types of noncompliance to be acceptable, and, second, whether they felt that noncompliance behavior in general may be justifiable (and if so, why?). Responses were measured on a six-point scale indicating strong agreement to strong disagreement.

A second set of compliance questions focuses on the *level* of noncompliance. This issue was addressed in two ways. First, the survey recorded respondents' own admitted past noncompliance behavior. Respondents were asked direct questions

---

[10] Another set of questions, discussed below, asked respondents how severely cheaters *should* be penalized.

TABLE 5
Taxpayer Opinion Survey—Attitudinal Sets Measured

Attitudes About the Tax System	Attitudes About Society
Effectiveness of Tax Reform	Respect for Authority
Equity in the distribution of taxes	Trust in Government
Risk of detection for evaders	Faith in Human Integrity
Penalties assessed on noncompliers	Disenfranchisement
Tax complexity	Need to take risks

TABLE 6

Taxpayer Opinion Survey—Specific Noncompliance Activities Discussed with Respondents

Are the following activities acceptable or unacceptable?

Unreported income from barter activities

Unreported income from secondary sources (second job, etc.)

Overstatement of deductions for expenses actually incurred

Unreported cash payments

Unreported investment income

Deduction of ineligible medical expenses

---

about whether they had previously cheated on their tax returns, and if so, how. If they admitted to underreporting income, they were asked about the kind of income they did not report. Other questions address the potential for overpayment of tax liability, and for nonintentional noncompliance. These questions are summarized in Table 8.

In recognition that some respondents may have been reluctant to admit to personal noncompliance behavior, another set of questions addressed respondents' perceptions of the level of noncompliance activity engaged in by others. Respondents were asked what percentage of other taxpayers they think cheat on their taxes, and by how much (i.e., are the amounts large or small?). Respondents were also asked about their perceptions of tax evasion trends: is cheating becoming more or less widespread?

A third dimension of the compliance issue was addressed with questions concerning respondents' sympathies for tax protestors and tax cheaters. Questions in this category asked respondents if they perceive a distinction between tax protestors and tax cheaters. Do tax protestors serve a useful purpose by focusing

---

TABLE 7

Taxpayer Opinion Survey—Respondent Sympathies For Noncompliance Rationalizations

In some circumstances, noncompliance may be justifiable because:

Need	Cost of living too high
Faith in gov't.	Government spends too much
Fairness	Many rich people don't pay their share
	Deduction is deserved, but not allowed
Human integrity	Others would cheat if they could
Risk	Unlikely to get caught
Uncertainty	Uncertainty should be resolved in taxpayer's own favor
Materiality	Respondent is otherwise a loyal & law-abiding citizen
	No one is really harmed by small levels of noncompliance

TABLE 8
Direct Measures of Noncompliance Activity

Activity	Responses
Failure to Take Legitimate Deductions:	Yes or no? Why? (ignorance, materiality, etc.)
Arithmetic Errors:	Notification of previous errors? Underpayment or overpayment?
Overstated Deductions:	Admitted overstatement?
Substantiation:	Deductions for unsubstantiated expenditures?
Underreported Income:	Admitted underreporting? Type? (cash payments, tips, etc.)

---

public attention on how the government spends money, or should they be considered criminals? What kind of people are tax cheaters (as opposed to tax protestors)? Are they just ordinary people unlucky enough, or dumb enough, to get caught? Are they inherently dishonest? Are most cheaters wealthy people trying to get away with paying less? Finally, a very interesting series of questions asked respondents how strong the penalties *should be* for tax evasion.

The final group of questions addressing noncompliance levels asked respondents for their insights into how noncompliance levels can most effectively be reduced. The survey contains open-ended questions asking respondents what things the IRS may be doing that *actually encourage people to cheat* on their taxes, and what it could do to discourage evasion. These questions are accompanied by a series of closed-end questions asking respondents whether certain specific activities might discourage cheating. These questions addressed activities ranging from increased media publicity of tax prosecutions, and increased imposition of jail sentences, to increased sharing of information between the IRS and other governmental agencies.

Evaluating the IRS. Much of the survey is devoted to obtaining feedback from respondents concerning how well the IRS performs its responsibilities. One entire segment of the survey focuses on respondents' "awareness of the IRS." Do respondents pay attention when the IRS is discussed in the media? Do they ever discuss the agency with family workers or co-workers? What is their primary source of information about the agency?

Other questions are more focused and address whether certain practices of the Service are beneficial or futile, and whether the agency generally does a competent job when dealing with the public. Questions in this category address whether respondents receive their tax forms on time, whether they rely on IRS personnel to complete their returns, and, if so, how they would evaluate the employees they deal with. In addition, respondents were asked whether they use the peel-off label, and the pre-addressed envelope, enclosed with their form booklets, and, if not, why not? Finally, a series of questions addresses the usefulness of IRS publications and the convenience of various sources for additional forms (post office, library, etc.).

Demographics. A variety of demographic variables are measured throughout the survey. These variables, summarized in Table 9, are largely self-explanatory (age, race, sex, education, income level, marital status, etc.), but some may need additional explanation. Occupational variables provide information on whether the respondent or spouse were self-employed, whether they worked full-time or part-time, or were unemployed at the date of the interview. In addition, the survey records the industry and type of job in which each respondent was employed, as well as whether the respondent worked more than one job.

Information on the respondents' opportunities to evade taxes is provided in the form of questions regarding sources of income (wages/salary, tips, sale of property, etc.). With regard to IRS contact, respondents were asked whether they or someone they knew had previously been contacted by the IRS, and, if so, what was the nature of the contact (notice of deficiency, audit, etc.)?

Several questions address the return preparation issue. The survey records whether respondents usually do their own returns, or usually have them done by someone else. For respondents using return preparers, the survey records the professional status of the preparer (accountant, lawyer, etc.), and the primary reason the respondents use a preparer (complexity, time, expertise of the preparer, etc.).

Three questions record whether the respondents owned their own home, whether the home had been refinanced, and whether the total debt exceeded the cost of the home plus improvements. Finally, a series of questions provides information on the type of return filed. Information is available regarding the type of form filed by each respondent (long or short form), the nature of attached schedules (C or F vs. other), and the respondent's itemizer status. The number and nature of dependents claimed by each respondent was also recorded.

Summing up, the 1987 *Taxpayer Opinion Survey* provides data on over 300 questions for 2,003 respondents. These questions focus on the respondents' admitted noncompliance activity as well as their perceptions of, and attitudes toward, the noncompliance activities of others. In addition, the survey measures a variety of variables which may be correlated with noncompliance activity, from demographic variables such as age and sex to environmental variables such as tax

---

TABLE 9
Taxpayer Opinion Survey—Demographic Variables Measured

Age	Income Level
Race	Opportunity to Evade
Affiliation with Community Organizations	Previous Contact with IRS
Type of Return Filed	Use of Professional Preparer
Sex	Homeowner?
Occupation & Employment Status	Marital Status
Education	No. of Dependents

complexity and opportunity to evade taxes. Clearly, with over 300 measured responses, many of these variables are measured using multiple questions. This leaves open the possibility that some questions may also reflect other factors not considered in the initial survey design. This possibility is one reason that the Service has made the data base publicly available to academic researchers from outside the government.

Data Limitations

The *Taxpayer Opinion Survey* provides another potentially rich source of information for researchers interested in tax compliance questions. Unlike the TCMP files, the opinion survey measures a variety of non-financial factors which may contribute to noncompliance. The survey can distinguish, for example, between taxpayers who feel that the system is unfair, and those who do not. It can also determine the extent to which taxpayers feel that the IRS is omnipotent, and that it is therefore very unlikely that they could get away with noncompliant behavior. Also, unlike the TCMP files, the opinion survey focuses on intentional noncompliance behavior and contains information on both filers and nonfilers. Thus, for many purposes, the opinion survey file may be a more useful data set than the TCMP files.

However, the survey does suffer from limitations. Chief among these is that it measures only *admitted* noncompliance. It is possible that survey measures of admitted noncompliance reflect a need by some respondents "to announce in a survey what [they've] done" rather than actual noncompliance activity (Yankelovich, Skelly and White 1984, 118). More likely, it is possible that some noncompliers are reluctant to admit to cheating, so that the survey may understate actual noncompliance levels. These limitations were recognized by the Service prior to commissioning the survey, of course, and it is possible that the measures of respondent attitudes toward noncompliance may serve as a better proxy of noncompliance behavior than do the measures of admitted noncompliance.

A second limitation of the survey is that, unlike in the TCMP, participation in the survey was voluntary. Thus, it is possible that the survey may suffer from nonresponse bias. If noncompliers were more likely than compliers to refuse to participate in the survey, then estimated noncompliance levels may be understated.

Data Access

Unlike the TCMP files, access to the *Taxpayer Opinion Survey* file is not restricted. The file is available on computer tape from the Office of Tax Policy Research at the University of Michigan. The tapes are stored in standard SAS format and are quite easily accessed. Cost of the file is $600.00. To order the file, contact:

> The Office of Tax Policy Research
> School of Business Administration
> University of Michigan
> Ann Arbor, MI 48109-1234
> (313) 936-0765

The Office of Tax Policy Research will provide the data and bill the researcher's university.

Alternatively, some researchers may be able to obtain the Survey File free of charge from the Inter-University Consortium for Political and Social Research (ICPSR). Researchers affiliated with member institutions of the ICPSR can obtain the file at no charge.[11] See the addendum to this chapter for information regarding the ICPSR.

SECTION 3: THE SURVEY OF TAX PRACTITIONERS AND ADVISERS

In May-July, 1986, the Service commissioned another nation-wide survey, this time of tax preparers and advisers. The *Survey of Tax Practitioners and Advisers* measured practitioners' attitudes toward the IRS, and their evaluations of IRS services. Other questions addressed the impact practitioners may have on client behavior, and how practitioners feel about signing questionable returns, or retaining questionable clients. Thus, this data base provides a source of information for analyzing yet another component of the compliance model.[12]

Overview of the Practitioner Survey

Purpose of the Survey. The *Survey of Tax Practitioners and Advisers* was motivated by two objectives. The first objective was external in nature; the Service wanted to gain some insight into the role of tax preparers in the compliance behavior of clients. Although the question of whether taxpayers using professional preparers are more or less likely to cheat on their taxes can be addressed directly using the TCMP file, the survey provides insights into the role of preparers. Do preparers implicitly or explicitly condone certain levels of noncompliance behavior? Do they advise their clients to participate in certain activities, and to avoid others? What standards, if any, do they require, with regard to compliance issues, in preparing and signing tax returns? And what are their own perceptions regarding their influences on client behavior?

In addition to exploring the compliance issue, the IRS wanted an evaluation of its performance. The second objective of the practitioner survey was to determine how IRS services, and IRS personnel, are rated by the Service's professional peers.

Sampling Procedure. The survey sample was drawn from the IRS preparer inventory and central authorization files. The preparer inventory file (PIF) contains the identification numbers of all preparers signing the paid preparer's block on tax returns. The central authorization file (CAF) contains identification numbers for all taxpayer representatives who have obtained powers of attorney to negotiate for their clients.

The primary focus of the survey was on return preparers. A stratified random sample of preparers was selected from the 1984 PIF and contacted by a professional

---

[11] The 1987 Taxpayer Opinion Survey is ICPSR Study No. 8927.

[12] See IRS (1987) for a summary of the Tax Preparer Survey results. Also see Jackson, Milliron and Toy (1988), and Jackson and Milliron (1989) for interesting critiques of the Service's interpretation of the results.

surveying firm. At the date of the survey, the PIF identified approximately 42,000,000 individual tax returns which had been signed by preparers. These returns (rather than the preparers themselves) were stratified in a manner similar to that described for the *Taxpayer Opinion Survey*, and a sample of preparers signing such returns was randomly selected. Thus, the initial sample was designed to be *representative of the entire population of tax returns prepared by professional preparers*. Professional preparers in the sample are weighted in accordance with the number of returns they prepared.

To be eligible for inclusion in the sample, preparers were required to satisfy two criteria. First, they (or their employees) must have signed at least five returns. Second, preparers were interviewed only if they signed returns in both 1984 and 1985. These restrictions, together with the inability to contact some preparers, or the unwillingness of some practitioners to participate, limited the study's response rate to around 50 percent. In all, a sample of 1,772 preparers participated in the study as summarized in Table 10. In addition, a separate sample of 152 lawyers was drawn from the IRS central authorization file and asked to answer the same questions. The two samples were maintained separately because it was anticipated by the Service that the latter group, representing *advisers* rather than preparers, might exhibit different characteristics than the former.

Data Available. The practitioner survey collected preparers' and advisers' responses to a 58 item questionnaire. As with the opinion survey, each item on the questionnaire was divided into subparts so that there are substantially more than 58 responses from each participant. In all, the data base contains responses to more than 300 questions for each of 1,772 tax return preparers and 152 tax advisers.

In general, the questions can be classified into 3 categories: (1) preparer/adviser behavior related to compliance and administration of the tax law, (2) preparer/adviser evaluation of the IRS, and (3) demographic information. The following is a general discussion of types of questions addressed in each category. For a more specific description of the survey, including a reproduction of the survey questionnaire, the reader should see *Survey of Tax Practitioners and Advisers: Summary of Results by Occupation* (IRS 1987).

TABLE 10
Samples for the 1986 Survey of Tax Practitioners

Sample	Professional Status	Sample Size
Tax Preparers	CPAs	688
	Enrolled Agents	202
	Attorneys	88
	Public Accountants	264
	Unenrolled Agents	530
	Total	1,772
Advisers	Attorneys signing returns	109
	Attorneys not signing returns	43
	Total	152

Table 11 provides an overview of the survey questions related to preparer/ adviser behavior. As indicated, the survey asked respondents about their behavior in six areas. The first area concerns audit risk. Respondents were asked how they would advise a client with regard to a deduction (e.g., home office expense) which might increase the risk that the client's return would be audited. Would they be conservative and advise against taking the deduction, or would they instead try to disguise the deduction to reduce the audit risk? A second area of behavior dealt with amended returns. Would respondents advise clients to file amended returns upon discovery of a preparer error? What if an estimated deduction was subsequently discovered to be in error?

The largest group of questions addressed the issue of practitioner complicity in overstating deductions or underreporting income. Here respondents were asked about their tenacity in searching for client transgressions and their willingness to sign returns when they suspect such behavior may be taking place. Additionally, respondents were asked whether they would warn a client of the potential consequences of intentional noncompliance.

The last two groups of questions deal with practitioner participation in the administration of the tax law. Respondents were asked how they dealt with items the proper treatment of which is uncertain, and how much investigation they do when asked by a client to prepare a delinquent return. Additionally, the survey asked respondents whether they compute penalties for underpayment of ES taxes for their clients, or wait to see if the IRS will compute the penalties and send a bill, and whether and how they use the IRS' internal appeals procedure.

TABLE 11
Practitioner Survey—Preparer Actions Discussed in Survey

Issue	Action
Audit Risk	Advise against deductions? Disguise deductions?
Amended Returns	Beneficial (to client) preparer errors? Costly (to client) preparer errors? Estimated expenses differ from actual?
Deductions	Signature when return contains shelters? Signature when return contains undocumented deduction? Signature when deductions not fully documented? "Stretch" allowable deductions?
Income	Extent of investigation for unreported income? Signature when client is suspected of underreporting income? Caution client about criminal penalties?
Other Reporting	Resolution of questionable items in client's favor? Attach computation of ES penalties? Inquiries regarding prior delinquent returns?
Dealing with IRS	Use of Appeals for delay? Use of Appeals as negotiating ploy?

For each of the actions discussed above, respondents were asked about four dimensions of practitioner behavior. First, would they *personally* behave in this way? Second, if so, how frequently have they previously engaged in a particular action? Third, what do they perceive the consequences to be if such behavior were detected by the IRS? Finally, what percentage of their peers do they feel would engage in such behavior? That is, how many *other* practitioners would advise their clients in a particular way, or would take certain actions on behalf of their clients? As with the *Taxpayer Opinion Survey*, the latter question is designed to serve as a surrogate for practitioner behavior as a safeguard against any potential reluctance by respondents to admit to their own transgressions.

A major portion of the survey was devoted to obtaining practitioner evaluations of the IRS. As summarized in Table 12, practitioners were asked to evaluate the IRS on a specific array of services and quality of administration issues. A thorough discussion of these evaluations is provided in White (1988) and in IRS (1987).

Data Limitations

The *Survey of Tax Practitioners and Advisers* is subject to many of the same limitations as the *Taxpayer Opinion Survey*. Most notably, to the extent the survey contains information about practitioner complicity in the noncompliance activities of clients, it must be remembered that such information is self-reported. As a result, it may understate the true noncompliant activities of some respondents, while other respondents may be exaggerating behavior in order to accomplish some unknown objective. As with the other survey, these problems may be partially alleviated by the inclusion of questions which indirectly attempt to measure the same behavior.

Additionally, it must be remembered that a sizable component of the sample did not participate in the sample due to unwillingness or the inability of the surveyors to locate selected practitioners. To the extent that the "nonrespondents" are not randomly distributed across the population (e.g., nonrespondents and respondents differ with regard to noncompliance behavior), then the survey may be subject to nonresponse bias. Results should be interpreted accordingly.

Data Access

The *Survey of Tax Practitioners and Advisers* data base is available from the Office of Tax Policy Analysis at the University of Michigan. The file is available on

---

TABLE 12
Practitioner Evaluations of IRS

General Attitudes Toward IRS

Ratings of Available IRS Information

Evaluation of IRS Toll-Free Taxpayer Advice System

Evaluation of Private Letter Ruling Program

Ratings of IRS Personnel

Evaluation of Problem Resolution Office

---

computer tape (in standard SAS format) at a cost of $600.00. Requests for the data should be sent to the address noted previously. Alternatively, for researchers at member institutions, this file is also available from the Inter-University Consortium for Political and Social Research.[13]

Summary and Concluding Remarks

This chapter has discussed three data tapes available to researchers interested in tax compliance issues. The TCMP files contain the most accurate information on noncompliance levels available, along with information on a variety of variables which may help to explain noncompliant behavior. But access to this data is restricted. Proposals must be approved by the IRS before access is granted, and research must be conducted jointly with the IRS.

In contrast, the survey files are accessible to anyone interested in purchasing them. Moreover, the survey files contain information on taxpayer and practitioner attitudes which is not available on the TCMP files. The tradeoff is that the information regarding noncompliance levels provided by the surveys may be less reliable than that provided by the TCMP files. Nonetheless, researchers interested in tax compliance should find the survey files to be an invaluable source of data for analyzing the relationship between compliance/noncompliance behavior and many attitudinal and demographic variables that are not directly measurable from tax return data.

ADDENDUM:
INTER-UNIVERSITY CONSORTIUM FOR POLITICAL AND SOCIAL RESEARCH (ICPSR)

Suzanne M. Luttman
Santa Clara University

An excellent and relatively inexpensive source of data is available for academic researchers whose employers are among the 360 members of the Inter-university Consortium for Political and Social Research (ICPSR). Faculty and students at member institutions pay only the cost of both the magnetic tape used to copy the data and any necessary documentation. Data can be obtained by individuals at non-member institutions only after a fee has been negotiated.

ICPSR classifies a database by its amount of processing: Class I (checked, corrected, formatted to standard ICPSR specifications, recoded and reorganized if necessary) to Class IV (distributed in the form received from the investigator). The processing decision is determined by the ICPSR advisory committee based on the perceived demand for the data. The ICPSR takes no responsibility for the technical condition of the data in Class IV.

---

[13] The Practitioner Survey is ICPSR Study No. 08884.

The *Guide to Resources and Services* describes the archival holdings of the ICPSR by general subject area. There is a one to two paragraph summary of each database. The ICPSR holdings are designed for social science research, so databases range in subject material from wars and conflicts to legal institutions; international databases are also available. Certain databases are updated continuously, and the ICPSR makes available all new versions of selected databases. For tax research, some of the most useful databases might be census data, surveys of economic behavior, health care, and social institutions and behavior. The following brief discussion of some databases and their content is provided to illustrate the type of data available through the ICPSR.

The *Annual Housing Survey* (by the Bureau of the Census) contains data on a national sample of housing units and a second sample of housing units in 20 standard metropolitan areas (SMSAs). Included is information on costs incurred for mortgage payments, real estate taxes, insurance, and utilities. Comparisons can be made between geographic regions or from year to year. Income data are also collected.

The *Current Population Survey* (also by the Bureau of the Census) gathers data primarily on labor force activity. Employment status, occupation, job tenure, occupational mobility, and employing industry are reported with the accompanying demographic information.

General Revenue Sharing information is made available by the Bureau of the Census, indicating the per capita money income for counties, the current population estimates, and the federal revenue sharing allocations.

The *Consumer Expenditure Survey* is used by the Bureau of Labor Statistics in part to maintain and review the Consumer Price Index. It provides information on purchases made by households (major items and small, frequently purchased items such as food), expenditures (such as taxes paid), and income and demographic information.

Consumer Durables and Installment Debt provides detailed answers to questions about family income, purchases of durables, current level of financial debt, asset holdings (for example, houses, savings and checking accounts, stocks and bonds).

The *Panel Study of Income Dynamics* is a longitudinal survey of economic status, economic behavior, and attitudes. Demographic (e.g., age, race, family status, education) and economic (e.g., income, employment, housing, asset ownership) questions are answered by the respondents and supplemental information (e.g., local wages, unemployment rates) is added by the interviewer.

The *National Longitudinal Surveys of Labor Market Experience* (Center for Human Resource Research, Ohio State University) provides a 20-year forum for analyzing sources of variation in labor market behavior. Information on minority, youth, and female (including fertility and child care) work experiences is provided.

The Social Security Administration merged Statistics of Income data with demographic information from its longitudinal summary earnings files, and these data are available in the *Augmented Individual Income Tax Model Exact Match File.*

As previously mentioned, the *1987 National Taxpayer Opinion Survey* and the *1986 Survey of Tax Practitioners and Advisers* are also available.

For additional information, contact:
Inter-university Consortium for Political and Social Research (ICPSR)
Institute for Social Research
P. O. Box 1248
Ann Arbor, MI 48106
(313) 763-5010

REFERENCES

Broehm, K., and K. Sharp. 1989. Summary of Public Attitude Survey Findings. *Trend Analyses and Related Statistics 1989 Update* (IRS): 65-77.

Clotfelter, C. 1983. Tax Evasion and Tax Rates: An Analysis of Individual Returns. *Review of Economics and Statistics* 45 (August): 363-73.

Chang, O., and J. Schultz. 1990. The Income Tax Withholding Phenomenon: Evidence from TCMP Data. *The Journal of the American Taxation Association* (Fall): 88-92.

Dubin, J., and S. Henson. 1988. The Distributional Effects of the Federal Energy Tax Act. *Resources and Energy* 10 (September): 191-212.

Feinstein, J. 1991. An Econometric Analysis of Income Tax Evasion and Its Detection. *Rand Journal of Economics* 22 (Spring): 14-35.

Internal Revenue Service. 1985. *Conference on Tax Administration Research — Proceedings.* Office of the Assistant Commissioner (Planning, Finance and Research).

———. 1986. *Trend Analyses and Related Statistics 1986 Update.* IRS Document 6011.

———. 1987. *Survey of Tax Practitioners and Advisers: Summary of Results by Occupation.* Office of the Assistant Commissioner (Planning, Finance and Research).

———. 1989. *Taxpayer Compliance Measurement Program Handbook.* Office of the Assistant Commissioner (Planning, Finance and Research).

Jackson, B., and V. Milliron. 1989. Tax Preparers: Government Agents or Client Advocates? *Journal of Accountancy* 167 (May): 76-82.

———, ———, and D. Toy. 1988. Tax Practitioners and the Government. *Tax Notes* (October 17): 333-341.

Louis Harris and Associates, Inc. 1987a. *1987 Taxpayer Opinion Survey.* IRS Document 7292.

———. 1987b. *1987 Taxpayer Opinion Survey Appendix, Trended Data: 1987, 1984 and 1966.* IRS Document 7293.

Madeo, S., A. Schepanksi, and W. Uecker. 1987. Modeling Judgments of Taxpayer Compliance. *The Accounting Review* (April): 323-42.

Slemrod, J. 1989. Are Estimated Tax Elasticities Really Just Tax Evasion Elasticities? The Case of Charitable Contributions. *Review of Economics & Statistics* 71 (August): 517-22.

White, Patricia. 1988. Paid Preparers' Rating of the IRS: Select Items from the 1986 Survey of Tax Practitioners. *Trend Analyses and Related Statistics 1988 Update* (IRS): 169-80.

Wilt, D., and S. Perng. 1988. The Importance of Unreported Income Probes on High DIF-Scored Returns. *Trend Analyses and Related Statistics 1988 Update* (IRS): 153-60.

Yankelovich, Skelly, and White, Inc. 1984. *Taxpayer Attitudes Study Final Report.* Internal Revenue Service.

Chapter 3
Sources of Corporate Tax Data

Much of the burden in performing tax research relates to gathering data. Prior research monograph chapters have focused on sources of data for research relating to individual taxpayers, as opposed to corporate taxpayers. However, tax problems that relate solely to corporations must also be addressed. So, where can we find data for corporate tax research? Obvious sources include companies' annual reports to stockholders and 10Ks filed with the SEC, but obtaining these documents for selected sample companies is sometimes difficult and time consuming.[1] Even if these documents are obtained, numerous man-hours are required to retrieve the pertinent data necessary for specific research projects. Fortunately, computer technology can alleviate some of these problems.

SECTION 1: COMPUSTAT

Danny P. Hollingsworth and Steven R. Rich
Baylor University

Standard and Poor's (S&P) produces *Compustat* files for both the mainframe computer and the personal computer (PC). These files constitute a computerized data base of financial, statistical, and market related data for a large number of companies. The PC version has a stock reports file, a corporate text file, and a financial data base. Stock reports include market data on stock prices as well as basic business information such as financial ratios and dividend data. The corporate text file has the complete text of Annual Reports, 10Ks, 10Qs, 20Fs, and Proxy Statements for major corporations that have filed such reports with the SEC since July 1987. The PC financial data base is generally the same as the mainframe data base, except the PC version may include additional information that is not included in some mainframe subscriptions packages.[2] The following discussion focuses on Compustat for the mainframe computer rather than the PC version.

Data items on the mainframe version of Compustat consist of information reported on Income Statements, Balance Sheets, Statements of Changes in Financial Position, some footnote data, and market facts on New York, American, Over-The-Counter, Regional, and Canadian Stock Exchange companies. This data base is updated frequently to provide researchers relatively current data as well as older data. Typically, data for a particular company is available on either an annual basis for 20 years (40 years of back data is available for some companies) or a quarterly

---

[1] The use of financial statement data in tax research has many weaknesses as discussed by Dworin (1985), Fiekowsky (1977), Spooner (1986), and Weiss (1979).

[2] The information includes business segment data, geographic data, and multiple SIC codes for some companies. For more information on the PC version of Compustat, contact Standard & Poor's Compustat Services, Inc., 1211 Avenue of the Americas, New York, NY 10020 (212) 512-4900.

basis for 48 quarters. Historical and restated data are provided when a company has been involved in an acquisition, has a change in accounting method, or has a discontinued operation. Information is entered into the data base on a standardized basis, except for accounting method, to assure comparability among companies and periods.

The Compustat data base is comprised of various files that separate the data into workable components. These files, along with a brief description, include the following.[3]

(1) *Primary Industrial File* - Contains over 800 companies from S&P's Industrial, Utilities, Transportation, and Financial Indexes and the largest companies on the New York and American Stock Exchanges.

(2) *Supplementary Industrial File* - Contains over 800 companies listed on other major stock exchanges.

(3) *Tertiary File* - Contains over 800 companies listed on the major stock exchanges plus 300 nonindustrial companies such as Banks, Insurance Companies, and Utilities in the same format as the industrial companies.

(4) *Over-The-Counter File* - Contains over 850 companies on the OTC exchange.

(5) *Full-Coverage File* - Contains over 4,800 companies that file with the SEC.

(6) *Industrial Research File* - Contains companies deleted from the above files due to merger, bankruptcy, or other reasons that make them inactive.

(7) *Price-Dividends-Earnings (PDE) File* - Contains industry indexes and market information for all, except Canadian, Compustat files.

(8) *PDE Research File* - Contains companies that have been deleted from the Price-Dividends-Earnings File for the reasons listed in (6) above.

(9) *Canadian File* - Annual file, reported in Canadian currency, of over 500 major Canadian companies.

(10) *Aggregate File* - Contains an aggregation of data items (e.g., net income) by industry group (approximately 275), such as the S&P 500 and the Dow Jones 30 Industrials.

(11) *Business Information File* - This is a subset of three files: Standard Industrial Classification (SIC) File, Industry Segment File, and the Geographic Segment File. Various information (e.g., Net Sales by geographic area) is provided based upon the organization of each file.

(12) *Bank File* - Contains data on approximately 150 banks in the United States.

(13) *Register On-Line File* - Computerized version of *S&P's Register of Corporations, Directors, and Executives*, which provides corporate statistics and profiles on approximately 45,000 public and private companies.

(14) *Telecommunications File* - Contains information on all telephone companies that file Form 10K with the SEC.

(15) *Utility File* - Provides various financial, statistical, and market information on approximately 300 Utility companies.

(16) *ZACKS Earnings Estimates File* - Contains estimates of EPS for approximately 2,500 companies.

---

[3] This information is contained in the introduction section of the *Industrial Compustat* reference manual.

The availability of these files depends upon the subscription package selected by the subscriber (e.g., universities).

Using Compustat Data in Tax Research

Researchers have used Compustat data to analyze a variety of tax research problems. These problems range from macro-economic issues that affect the aggregate corporate sector to micro-tax issues that focus on how tax laws affect individual companies. Some studies use sophisticated models to statistically analyze the Compustat data, while others use the data to provide descriptive information about particular companies or industries. The following examples of studies using Compustat are far from exhaustive and is simply a nonrandom sample to illustrate the use of Compustat in tax research.

Effective Tax Rate Models. Bernard and Hayn (1986) used Compustat data to determine the effects that inflation has on a cross-sectional distribution of the corporate tax burden. This study used multiple regression to analyze company-specific *real effective tax rates* to test whether failure to index the tax system for the effects of inflation is largely offset by other features of the tax law (e.g., accelerated depreciation). The effective tax rate was defined by Bernard and Hayn as follows.

$$\text{Real Effective Tax Rate} = \frac{\text{Federal, State, and Foreign Income Taxes Currently Payable}}{\text{Real Distributable Profit}}$$

As noted by the authors, information in the numerator was not publicly disclosed by many corporations in earlier years (e.g., 1972), and thus, it was not directly available from Compustat. However, the authors demonstrate how items that are available on Compustat can be used to compute the desired information (i.e., income tax currently payable).

Income Tax Currently Payable =
    Total Income Tax Expense
    –   Net Deferred Income Tax Expense
    –   Tax Benefit of NOL Carryforward
    + or – Adjustment for Firms with Unconsolidated Subsidiaries

This study analyzed the *real effective tax rate* for 136 U.S. corporations from 27 different industries for the years 1961 through 1984. Imagine the amount of work and time it would take to compute this tax rate from corporate annual reports to stockholders or 10Ks filed with the SEC.

In a study similar to Bernard and Hayn (1986), Bruttomesso and Ketz (1982) used Compustat to examine the effect of inflation on corporate tax rates. They expanded a study by Davidson and Weil (1975), which found a substantial variation between historical cost tax rates and tax rates computed using techniques that considered the effect of inflation. Bruttomesso and Ketz examined tax rates of 112 companies from seven industries from 1959 to 1977. These companies and years were selected because of their availability on Compustat. Tax rates were computed three ways: one using historical cost data and two using general price level adjusted data. These tax rates are as follows.

$$\text{Historical Cost Tax Rate} = \frac{\text{Historical Cost Tax Expense}}{\text{Historical Cost Net Income Before Taxes}}$$

$$\text{General Price Level Tax Rate \#1} = \frac{\text{General Price Level Adjusted Tax Expense}}{\text{Pretax General Price Level Net Income, Without Monetary Gains and Losses}}$$

$$\text{General Price Level Tax Rate \#2} = \frac{\text{General Price Level Adjusted Tax Expense}}{\text{Pretax General Price Level Net Income, With Monetary Gains and Losses}}$$

The general price adjustments were obtained by using the Parker (1977) model, which is linked to the Compustat data base. Compustat was a logical source for data relating to general price level changes because such information was included in the companies' financial reports. Thus, when tax research uses information relating to corporate financial reports, Compustat is a viable option.

Wilkie (1988) also used Compustat to obtain data for computing corporate average effective tax rates (ETRs). The *Tax Analysts' Effective Corporate Tax Rates* data base had to be used in conjunction with Compustat to obtain the total data needed to conduct the study. The purpose of this study was to develop and test a model that explains differences or changes in ETRs. The tax rate was computed for this study as follows.

$$\text{ETR} = \frac{[\text{PTI} - \text{TP}] \times \text{T}}{\text{PTI}}$$

where;

TP = Tax Preferences (i.e., items that cause a difference in pre-tax accounting income and taxable income);

PTI = Pre-tax Accounting Income;

T = Tax Rate.

Wilkie selected a sample of 488 firms common to both data bases for the five-year period 1980-84. Since the *Tax Analysts' Effective Corporate Tax Rates* data base was the smaller of the two data bases,[4] it was apparently the controlling source of data. Deletions from the Tax Analysts' data base were necessary because some firms had negative income and other firms were not available from Compustat. This illustrates one of Compustat's restrictions: some companies are either not available or do not have information for the desired years. Researchers should consider the implications of using Compustat (with its coverage and missing data) for their particular study.

---

[4] Wilkie (1988), p. 80 notes that the *Tax Analysts'* data base contained 527 firms over the five-year period 1980-1984. The Compustat Industrial file contained at least 700 companies with some information during the period 1965-1984.

Using multiple data sources is typically driven by the model selected for the research. Wilkie's model, as described above, required the use of 22 tax preferences ranging from accelerated depreciation to unrepatriated foreign earnings. These tax preferences were obtained from the Tax Analysts' data base. To control for cross-firm and through-time differences in size, additional company size variables were categorized by income and tax preference. However, Wilkie (1988, 82) noted that measures of firm size (e.g., total assets, stockholder's equity, and market value of common equity) could be obtained from Compustat.

Shevlin (1987) used Compustat to supplement other data sources (e.g., prospectuses, financial statements, and 10Ks) to examine factors favoring the use of limited partnerships to finance research and development (R&D). One factor examined was the marginal tax rate of firms conducting R&D. Shevlin predicted that low marginal tax-rate firms were more likely than high marginal tax-rate firms to fund their R&D through limited partnerships, because low-rate firms could not fully take advantage of the tax benefits associated with R&D costs. By using limited partnerships to fund R&D activities, firms could pass the tax benefits on to high-tax rate taxpayers.

The 1984 Compustat Industrial and OTC files as well as other sources were used to gather data on 103 firms using limited partnerships to fund R&D activities. In addition, the 1984 Compustat Industrial and OTC files were used to gather data on firms with non-zero R&D expense, which represented a comparison group that financed R&D in-house. Shevlin's results generally found support for the hypothesis that low marginal tax-rate firms were more likely to use limited partnerships to fund R&D costs than high tax-rate firms, although the results were sensitive to the measurement of corporate tax rate.

Shevlin (1990) also used Compustat data in another study that sought to determine how corporate marginal effective tax rates are effected by net operating losses (NOLs) and future taxable income. The results show that the presence of NOLs produce marginal tax rates for firms that differ from the top statutory corporate tax rate. Marginal tax rate was defined as the change in the present value of the cash flow paid to (or recovered from) the tax authorities as a result of earning one extra dollar of taxable income in the current period. A stratified random sample of 200 firms from the 1987 Compustat Annual Industrial and OTC files was used to estimate marginal tax rates for 1975. Shevlin noted that although Compustat provides a large body of data that is readily available, the data is based on reported financial statement information, rather than tax filings, which makes its application to tax questions difficult. For this study taxable income had to be estimated from financial income and financial statement NOLs had to be adjusted to represent tax NOLs.

As demonstrated by Shevlin, Compustat data can be used for tax research even though the data is oriented toward financial accounting. It may be necessary for researchers to estimate various tax variables or supplement Compustat data with information from other sources, but Compustat should not be disregarded because it is based on financial accounting numbers. In addition to the above studies, there are many other effective tax rate studies that use financial data found on Compustat. Two recent studies include Omer, Molloy, and Ziebart (1991) and Shevlin and Porter

(1992). Omer, Molloy, and Ziebart study alternative measures of ETRs and Shevlin and Porter reexamine the results and inferences made by the Citizens for Tax Justice.

Tax Research Relating To Specific Industries. Compustat is useful when a tax law affects some industries more than others since companies are categorized according to their SIC codes. Halperin and Lanen (1987) used Compustat to determine whether the Supreme Court's ruling in *Thor Power Tool*[5] affected companies' choices of inventory valuation methods for financial reporting purposes. The court's decision in *Thor* prohibits firms from using a formula write-down procedure to determine market values of inventory under the lower-of-cost or market (LCM) method of accounting for inventories. This decision led some to believe that firms affected by the change in tax law would switch to the LIFO method of valuing inventory. Halperin and Lanen identified specific industries on Compustat that would be significantly affected by the court's decision, and therefore, candidates for switching to LIFO.

The study empirically tested whether a firm switching to LIFO at the time *Thor* became effective was associated with the classification of that firm as being affected by the *Thor* decision. Compustat allowed the researchers to identify firms' inventory methods as either LIFO or non-LIFO via inventory codes. Since the *Thor* decision was in 1979, a switch to LIFO shortly thereafter by an affected firm would be consistent with the *Thor* decision influencing the switch to LIFO. The results were consistent with the hypothesis that firms react to changes in the tax law by changing the way economic events are reported.

Corporate Behavior Influenced By Taxation. Many tax laws are enacted to encourage certain behavior among taxpayers. Much of this behavior is socially oriented, such as contributing to retirement plans or incurring expenditures relating to research and development (R&D). A corporation's financial reports are a rich source of information with respect to how a corporation behaves in response to various tax legislation.

Corporate pension plans have been accorded very favorable tax treatment for a number of years. A pension plan is the only savings vehicle in which contributions to it are tax deductible while its earnings are exempt from tax. Such tax treatment provides an incentive for corporations to engage in tax arbitrage by overfunding their pension plans. Compustat has been used as a source of data by Friedman (1982), Bodie, Light, Morck, and Taggart (1984), Francis and Reiter (1987), and Thomas (1988); all of which empirically investigated the relationship between the level of pension funding and a firm's tax status. High tax status firms (i.e., firms having a high tax burden) were predicted to have a greater incentive to over fund their pension plan than were low tax status firms.

Thomas (1988) used four separate tests to examine the relationship between a firm's tax status and its pension funding policy. In determining tax status, Thomas (using Compustat) classified firm-years according to whether the firm reported positive tax payments (high tax status) or reported tax losses that were either carried

---

[5] *Thor Power Tool Company v. Comm.*, 99 SCt. 773 (1979).

back to recover prior year taxes (intermediate tax status) or carried forward to offset future income (lowest tax status). Two tests examined the time-series behavior of pension flows for the period 1980-1984 to determine if a change in tax status resulted in a change in pension funding. The sample (677 companies) for these tests included all firms on the 1984 Compustat Expanded Annual Industrial and OTC tapes, after deleting certain industries (e.g., defense contractors and public utilities) that had non-tax incentives to over fund their pension plans. Two additional tests were used to examine the cross-sectional relation between tax status and pension funding. These tests involved a matched-pair design in which 90 high-tax firms were matched with 90 low-tax firms to analyze pension funding levels. Data for 1981 obtained from Compustat and the Department of Labor were used for this analysis. The results provide evidence that pension funding and tax status are related.

Eisner, Albert, and Sullivan (EAS) (1984) used Compustat to analyze the incentive effects relating to the incremental tax credit for R&D expenditures enacted by the Economic Recovery Tax Act of 1981 (ERTA). The empirical analysis for this study used 592 Compustat companies with information on R&D expenditures for 1980, 1981, and 1982 and taxes for 1981 and 1982. The methodology used by EAS was to analyze the profiles of companies that had R&D expenditures during the three-year period. The researchers note that only two classes of firms that had R&D expenditures could not receive R&D tax credits; those whose R&D expenditures did not exceed their base level,[6] and those that did not have a federal income tax liability. Compustat made it possible to determine what proportion of the 592 firms incurring R&D expenditures were not eligible for the tax credit. For example, in 1982 47.4 percent of qualified R&D expenditures was undertaken by firms not eligible for the credit.

Research On Tax Systems Other Than Federal Income Tax. As evidenced by the tax literature, most tax research is related to the Federal income tax system. However, a typical corporation must pay many different types of tax, ranging from employment taxes (e.g., State and Federal unemployment insurance) to state sales and use tax. Using Compustat, Schmidt (1986) studied the apportionment of multijurisdictional corporate income for state income tax purposes and Crum (1985, 1991) studied alternatives to value-added tax (VAT) collections.

Schmidt's study focused on the problem of equitably determining each state's share of a multijurisdictional corporation's (MJC) income. States typically use one of three methods to apportion MJC income: (1) separate accounting, (2) specific allocation, and (3) formulary apportionment. Schmidt reports the results from an empirical analysis of eleven apportionment formulas. The three variables used in the formulas to apportion MJC income to a particular state were: property cost, payroll expense, and sales. The relationship between these three variables and a firm's income was analyzed using a multiple regression procedure. The model Schmidt tested is as follows:

---

[6] The R&D tax credit as enacted by ERTA was incremental in nature to encourage firms to increase their R&D expenditures. Thus, each firm had a base level of R&D expenditures that had to be exceeded before it was eligible for the tax credit. This base level shifted from year to year. For example, the base for 1982 was the mean of qualified R&D expenditures of 1980 and 1981.

$$Y_{it} = a + b_1X_{1it} + b_2X_{2it} + b_3X_{3it} + e_{it}$$

where:

Y_{it} = net operating income of firm i for time t;

a = intercept term;

b_k = partial regression coefficients (k=1,2,3);

X_{1it} = gross property of firm i for time t;

X_{2it} = payroll expense of firm i for time t;

X_{3it} = sales of firm i for time t;

e_{it} = error term.

Compustat was used to gather data on 252 sample companies from 27 industries. To simulate multijurisdictional operations, companies were pooled together by industry to represent a multistate unitary group, with company-specific variable values representing state-specific values. Thus, the actual income of a company was a benchmark for comparing income derived from the apportionment formulas tested. The financial variables, as described in the multiple regression model, for each sample company were constructed by using various Compustat data items. Schmidt (1986, 24) explains this process as follows:

> Apportionable income consisted of item 13 (operating income) minus item 14 (depreciation) minus item 15 (interest expense) plus item 62 (interest income). Two property factors were constructed—gross property and net property. Gross property consisted of item 7 (gross plant) plus item 3 (inventories) plus eight times item 47 (rental expense) minus item 73 (construction in progress). Net property was computed by substituting item 8 (net plant) for item 7. Beginning and year-end balances were averaged for plant, inventories, and construction in progress. The sales factor was constructed by adding items 12 (net sales) and 62 (interest income). Finally, two measures of the payroll factor were computed. Payroll expense consisted of item 42 (labor and related expense) minus item 43 (pension and retirement expense). Number of employees was computed by averaging the beginning and year-end balances of item 29 (employees).

Schmidt found that property, payroll, and sales factors as used in the apportionment formula significantly represent a company's income-generating process. Even though the factors were found to be stable over time, they were not stable across industries.

Crum (1985) used a combination of the Industrial Compustat tapes and corporate annual reports to gather data for a study that investigated cash flow remittances of 24 different VAT forms. A sample of 47 large U.S. industrial companies representing 38 different industries were randomly selected from Compustat firms that reported the required data for the years 1978-1982. Using VAT forms from other countries, Crum utilized a simulation methodology to identify the major factors that have the most influence on VAT remittances. The results of the simulation indicate that the treatment of capital assets and exports by a VAT system has a significant revenue effect. In addition, the results found that different collection methods and inventory recognition procedures have little effect on revenue.

Crum performed another study in 1991 relating to VAT cash flow effects. In this study Crum selected a sample of 92 U.S. companies from Industrial Compustat Files and corporate annual reports to investigate the variation in financing costs among companies under different VAT forms and how such costs correlate with the capital intensity of the companies. The sample was selected from all U.S. companies on the Industrial Compustat File that reported the required data for years 1977-82. However, over-the-counter companies, utilities, banks, insurance companies, real estate trusts, and companies experiencing asset growth through merger or acquisitions that exceeded ten percent were excluded. Crum reports that total labor cost (Compustat Item #42) and short-term rate of interest (Compustat Item #105) were the most critical items for a company to be included in the sample because these items were not required disclosures.

Financing neutrality of different VAT forms has important tax policy implications because of the cash flow problems or benefits for companies subject to VAT. The results indicate that companies could have experienced either a financing benefit or burden during the 1978-82 time period, depending on which form of VAT was adopted. In addition, the form of VAT can affect capital-intensive companies differently than noncapital-intensive companies, which could create problems for the companies and economic growth in general.

Data Available On Compustat

Compustat categorizes company-specific financial information into annual and quarterly data items. For example, Annual Data Item #1 that is found on the Primary Industrial File is Cash and Short-term Investments. The content of data items range from very specific information such as Convertible Debt (Item #79) to a combination of other data items such as Cash and Short-term Investments (Data Item # 1), which is a combination of Cash (Item # 162) and Short-term Investments (Item # 163). It is important to know when a data item is a combination of several other data items, since there could be an overlap of information.

In addition to Data Items, Compustat employs a footnoting system that provides supplemental information for certain data items. But Compustat's footnotes do not correspond to information contained in Notes to Financial Statements typically found in a company's annual report to stockholders. For example, the detailed breakdown of information (e.g., major deferred tax items) found in the tax note to financial statements is not available on Compustat. Footnote information provided by Compustat is available for both annual and quarterly data items. A two-character reference code indicates:

(1) The data for a fiscal year reflects a change from previous years' data due to an accounting change, discontinued operation and/or acquisition;
(2) A particular data item is inconsistent with the Compustat definition due to the company's method of reporting;
(3) The accounting method used by the company in calculating certain key items such as accumulated depreciation, inventories, or earnings per share for the financial statements.[7]

---

[7] *Industrial Compustat*, Section 8-C, p. 14.

Data items, including footnotes, are defined in Compustat's reference manuals in alphabetical order. Typical information provided for a given data item include: a brief description of the item, a list of specific accounts or related information included in the data item, a list of items excluded from the data item, whether the data item is also combined with any other data items, industries or company groups (e.g., banks, insurance companies, utilities) for which the data item is not available, and the annual or quarterly footnote code and related footnote description. These data definitions apply to both annual and quarterly data, unless the description indicates otherwise. Occasionally a data item will only apply to quarterly information, in which case, the definition will contain a QTR reference to indicate that it pertains to only quarterly data.

In addition to the actual data items as historically reported, Compustat contains data items that are restated for up to ten years as a result of acquisitions, accounting changes, and/or discontinued operations when such information is reported by the firm. Restated data items are only available for annual data as reported by firms and are presented on a basis comparable to current year information. Tax researchers should carefully consider which series of data (i.e., historical or restated) is most appropriate in their setting if restated data is available. When using a restated data item, users should compare the restated definition with the historical definition to assure that the data items are comparable.

After selecting a data item and analyzing its definition, users should determine if the data item is available for the desired year. Data items on Compustat have different origination dates. For example, Data Item #16, Income Taxes-Total, dates back to 1950, whereas Data Item #211, Income Taxes-Other, only goes back to 1984. Compustat's reference manuals contain a section (e.g., section 8-A in the Industrial Reference Manual) that provides the first year of data availability. This section also presents the display units (i.e., thousands and millions) and character precision (e.g., 10.3, which indicates ten characters, including the decimal, with the decimal located three characters to the left) for the data item.

In addition to data items that contain company-specific financial data, Compustat provides other company information that may be useful in tax research. A brief description of this information, including Compustat's mnemonic reference, for annual data on the Primary Industrial File is found below.[8]

Industry Classification Code (DNUM) - DNUM is a four-digit number that corresponds to the SIC code for the industry that best describes the company's business and product line as presented in Form 10k that is filed with the SEC.

Industry Name (INAME) - Compustat provides a standard name that corresponds to the Industry Classification Code.

CUSIP Issuer Code (CNUM) - This is a unique six-digit character code assigned by the CUSIP Service Bureau, New York, that identifies each company on Compustat.

Company Name (CONAME) - A brief name is assigned to each company that corresponds to a specific CUSIP Issuer Code (CNUM).

---

[8] *Industrial Compustat*, Section 8-B.

CUSIP Issue Number (CIC) - Specific issues of companies are identified by this three-character code.

File Identification Code (FILE) - Compustat uses this two-character code to specify the file (e.g., Primary Industrial, Tertiary, Aggregate) on which a company is located.

Exchange Listing and S&P Index Code (ZLIST) - This two-digit code indicates the stock exchange (e.g., New York) and the S&P Index Group (e.g., Utilities) in which a particular company participates.

Stock Ticker Symbol (SMBL) - The code represents the common stock ticker symbol used for publicly traded companies.

Fiscal Yearend Month of Data (FYR) - Compustat uses this two-digit code to indicate the month in which a company's fiscal year ends. Fiscal years ending between January 1 and May 31 are deemed to end in the *previous* calendar year.

Data Year (YEAR) - This is a code representing the last two digits of a given year (e.g., 1991) for which data is presented. Data Year may be any 12-month period representing the company's fiscal year. As noted in FYR above, years ending between January 1 and May 31 are treated as ending in the previous calendar year.[9]

S&P Industry Index Relative Code (XREL) - Companies may be included in either the S&P Industrial Index, the S&P Utilities Index, the S&P Transportation Index, the S&P Financial Index, or the S&P Supplementary Groups. XREL is a four-digit code that identifies the S&P industry group in which a company is included.

Stock Ownership Code (STK) - A one-digit STK code that identifies how a company's stock may be held: 0 - publicly traded, 1 - subsidiary of publicly traded company, 2 - subsidiary of non-publicly traded company, 3 - company that is publicly traded, but not on a major stock exchange.

Duplicate File Code (DUP) - This is a two-digit code that indicates other Compustat files that contains the company.

Update Code (UCODE) - Company information may be at different stages of completeness. This code represents the current status of a company's data. For example, UCODE 2 indicates the data has been updated from a preliminary source and some data may be incomplete.

Company Location Identification Code-State (STATE) - The state in which a company is located is identified by a two-digit STATE code. A 99 STATE code indicates the company is located outside the United States.

Company Location Identification Code-County (COUNTY) - Counties within a state are identified by a three-digit code. The COUNTY code must be used in conjunction with a STATE code to be meaningful.

Incorporation Code-Foreign (FINC) - This code identifies the country in which a company is incorporated. For example, FINC code 00 indicates a U.S. corporation.

---

[9] Researchers need to be very careful when using other data sources in conjunction with Compustat so that data years are consistent between the two data sources.

Source Document Code (SOURCE) - Since company information is updated from different sources, Compustat provides a two-digit SOURCE code that indicates the most recent source (e.g., prospectus) from which data were obtained.

Employer Identification Number (EIN) - All companies that operate within the U.S. must have a Federal Tax Identification Number. The EIN code represents this number. The first two digits of the Federal Tax Identification Number indicate the IRS district where the taxpayer was located when the number was issued.

Although the above descriptions relate to the *annual* format tapes, comparable information (e.g., S&P Bond Rating) is available for the *quarterly* format tape in the Compustat manuals.

Procedures For Accessing Compustat Data[10]

Accessing Compustat data can take several forms, depending on the computer storage capacity available. If disk space is limited, a subsample file that consists only of the desired data should be created directly from the Compustat data tape. However, if space allows, a more efficient approach is to read the data tapes into permanent SAS data sets. Research specific subsamples can then be created from these permanent SAS data sets. This second approach can reduce access time for the individual researcher from 3 to 4 hours down to 15 to 20 seconds. Sample programs for these two approaches are given in the appendices and are discussed below. In both programs, missing variable values are converted from .0001 (Compustat's code for data that is not available) to a single decimal point "." (the standard SAS system missing value code). Since these programs are written in SAS (version 6) they should require little modification for use on different computers and operating systems. However, job control language (JCL) and other file access procedures will differ between systems.

Creating Subsamples Directly from the Compustat Tapes. Subsamples can be created directly from the Compustat tapes with the sample program given in appendix A. This sample program will read the 360/370 general tape format versions of the annual industrial and industrial research Compustat tapes (e.g., primary, supplementary, tertiary, over-the-counter, etc.). A sample program for reading the Bank Files is available upon request. The sample program will create a permanent SAS data set named "SUBSAMP.DAT".

Two changes will need to be made in order to use the sample program. First, the fileref "CMPUSTAT" in the INFILE statement must have been previously associated with the external Compustat file to be read. See the SAS language manual for instructions on how this can be accomplished on a particular computer. Second, the variables, firms, industries, and/or years to be included in the subsample must be specified. For example, to create a subsample containing company names (CONAME), CUSIP Issuer Codes (CNUM), and pretax income (data item # 170) for IBM (IBM's CUSIP is 459200) for the year 1982, change:

---

[10] This section is written primarily for researchers at universities that have not established procedures for accessing Compustat tapes. Researchers at universities that have established procedures should contact their database managers or other computer personnel

```
KEEP XXX XXX XXX;
IF YEAR GE XX AND YR LE XX THEN OUTPUT;
```

to:

```
KEEP CONAME CNUM V170;
IF YEAR EQ 82 AND CNUM EQ '459200' THEN OUTPUT;
```

Note that CNUM is character data.

Creating Subsamples from Permanent SAS Data Sets. Creating subsamples from permanent SAS data sets stored on disk involves three steps. First, the Compustat files must be read into permanent SAS data sets using the sample program in appendix B. Second, these files should be indexed for faster access. Third, subsamples are created from the permanent SAS data set using the subsample program in appendix C.[11] The disk requirements for creating permanent SAS data sets for selected data files are given below:

Compustat Data File	Disk Space Needed (Megabytes)
Bank	5
Over-the-Counter	30
Over-the-Counter Research	30
Primary-Supplementary-Tertiary	80
Primary-Supplementary-Tertiary Research	55

Permanent SAS data sets can be created from the Compustat tapes with the program in appendix B. This program is also written to read the 360/370 general tape format versions of the annual industrial and industrial research Compustat tapes and will create a permanent SAS data set "ANNUAL.XXX". The first part of this label is the library name. The second part of the label should be changed to reflect the particular annual tapes data that is being read into the file. For example, if the Compustat tape being read is the Over-the-counter tape, the name might be changed from "ANNUAL.XXX" to "ANNUAL.OTC". In order to use this program, the fileref "CMPUSTAT" in the INFILE statement must have been associated with the external file to be read (see SAS language manual).

Indexing the data sets is very simple and reduces access time considerably. For example, to index the Over-the-counter (ANNUAL.OTC) and Over-the-counter research (ANNUAL.OTCR) data sets by CNUM, DNUM, and YEAR, run the following SAS statements:

```
PROC DATASETS LIBRARY=ANNUAL;
    MODIFY OTC;
        INDEX CREATE CNUM DNUM YEAR;
    MODIFY OTCR;
        INDEX CREATE CNUM DNUM YEAR;
```

---

[11] Alternatively, subsamples can be created with a merge statement. This can be accomplished by creating a separate SAS data set containing the desired Cusips, Years, etc. This file is then match-merged with the Compustat data set using an "In =" statement. The drawback to this approach is that the Compustat data set must first be sorted according to the "by" variables. The space required for such a sort is approximately double the disk space requirements listed below.

Subsets can be created from the permanent SAS data sets by using the program in appendix C. The subsample program allows for easy creation of subsamples of the data in several ways. Subsamples may be created containing specific variables, firms, years, firms from particular industries, or combinations thereof.

Subsamples are created by CNUM, DNUM, or YEAR by removing the "*" from before the desired selection criteria and making needed adjustments.

Examples:

1. To access IBM for all years, change:

    *   WHERE CNUM EQ '449842' OR CNUM EQ '755078';
    *   WHERE CNUM BETWEEN '000001' AND'002000';

    to:

          WHERE CNUM EQ '459200';
    *   WHERE CNUM BETWEEN '000001' AND '002000';

    Note:

      - Be sure to include the single quotation marks since CNUM is a character variable.
      - Do not eliminate the ; at the end of the statement.

2. To access all firms for all years in the Paper and Paper Products-Wholesale industry, change:

    *   WHERE DNUM EQ 0800 OR DNUM EQ 1000;
    *   WHERE DNUM BETWEEN 0200 AND 1040;

    to:

          WHERE DNUM EQ 5110;
    *   WHERE DNUM BETWEEN 0200 AND 1040;

3. To include all firms for the years 1987 through 1990, change:

    *   WHERE YEAR EQ 79 OR YEAR EQ 83;
    *   WHERE YEAR BETWEEN 86 AND 90;

    to:

    *   WHERE YEAR EQ 79 OR YEAR EQ 83;
          WHERE YEAR BETWEEN 87 AND 90;

To create subsamples with more than one set of criteria at a time, simply change the "WHERE" to "WHERE SAME AND" for all where statements after the first one.

Example: Suppose you wish to access data for IBM for the year 1986, then change:

    *   WHERE CNUM EQ '449842' OR CNUM EQ '755078';
    *   WHERE CNUM BETWEEN '000001' AND '002000';

    to:

          WHERE CNUM EQ '459200';
    *   WHERE CNUM BETWEEN '000001' AND '002000';

    and change:

    *   WHERE YEAR EQ 79 OR YEAR EQ 83;
    *   WHERE YEAR BETWEEN 86 AND 90;

to:

> WHERE SAME AND YEAR EQ 86;
> * WHERE YEAR BETWEEN 87 AND 90;

One of the best ways to limit the size of a subsample is to keep only selected variables. To use this part of the subsample program, remove the "*" from before the KEEP statement and adjust the keep list as necessary.

Example:

> To create a subsample including company name, CNUM, YEAR, V2, and V259, change:
>
> * KEEP CNUM YEAR V1-V12;
>
> to:
>
> KEEP CONAME CNUM YEAR V2 V259;

The Compustat permanent SAS data sets are basically flat files that appear as follows:

CNUM	Date	V1	V2
•	•	•	•
003443	88	302.33	22.34
003443	89	312.33	23.34
003443	90	289.46	19.99
1097B4	71	12.33	3.33
1097B4	72	9.78	2.45
•	•	•	•

As a result, care must be taken when lagging variables. Otherwise, lagging V1 will result in a lagged value of 289.46 for firm 1097B4 for the year 1971. This is obviously incorrect since 289.46 is the value of V1 for firm 003443 for 1990. Therefore, the safest way to create lagged data values is to use the subsample program.

Steps:
1. Remove the "*" from the beginning of all three lag statements.
2. Change VXXX to the variable to be lagged.
3. Change "KEEP" statement (if used) to include the lagged variable.
4. If more than one variable is to be lagged, duplicate the last two statements as necessary.

Example: To lag V32 and V49, change:

```
*    CNUML1 = LAG1 (CNUM);
*    VXXXL1 = LAG 1 (VXXX);
*        IF CNUML1 NE CNUM THEN VXXXL1 = .;
```

to:

```
CNUML1 = LAG1 (CNUM);
V32L1 = LAG1 (V32);
    If CNUML1 NE CNUM THEN V32L1 = .;
V49L1 = LAG1 (V49);
    IF CNUML1 NE CNUM THEN V49L1 = .;
```

If the keep variables statements is also being used, then the keep list must be changed to include the lagged variables.

Example:

KEEP CONAME CNUM YEAR V32 V49 V260;

to:

KEEP CONAME CNUM YEAR V32 V49 V260 V32L1 V49L1;

To lag a variable for more than one period, create the following statements and change XXX to the desired variable:

```
CNUML2 = LAG2 (CNUM);
VXXXL2 = LAG2 (VXXX);
        IF CNUML2 NE CNUM THEN VXXXL2 = .;
```

Occasionally, firms with missing values for certain variables for any of the years in the sample needs to be excluded from the dataset. This can be accomplished by using the last part of the subsample program. To use, remove the /* before PROC SQL and the */ at the end of the program then change the variable list as necessary.

Example: Suppose you wish to exclude any firm that has a missing value for V79 for any year, then change:

```
/* PROC SQL;
CREATE TABLE SASDAT.NOMISS AS
        SELECT * FROM SASDAT.SUBSAMPL
            WHERE CNUM NOT IN
                (SELECT DISTINCT CNUM FROM SASDAT.SUBSAMPL
                    WHERE    (V1   IS MISSING OR
                              V2   IS MISSING OR
                              V3   IS MISSING OR
                              V4   IS MISSING OR
                              V5   IS MISSING OR
                              V6   IS MISSING OR
                              V7   IS MISSING OR
                              V8   IS MISSING OR
                              V9   IS MISSING OR
                              V10  IS MISSING OR
                              V11  IS MISSING OR
                              V12  IS MISSING) ); */
```

to:

```
PROC SQL;
CREATE TABLE SASDAT.NOMISS AS
        SELECT * FROM SASDAT.SUBSAMPL
            WHERE CNUM NOT IN
                (SELECT DISTINCT CNUM FROM SASDAT.SUBSAMPL
                    WHERE (V79 IS MISSING) );
```

Concluding Remarks On Compustat

Compustat files represent a rich source of corporate data for tax researchers. This paper briefly explains what Compustat files include, it illustrates how

Compustat has been used in tax research, it describes the data available on Compustat files, and it provides some procedures for accessing Compustat data. Compustat is particularly useful for obtaining data on relatively large companies in which their stock is traded on a public stock exchange. Annual data for 20 years (40 years in some cases) or quarterly data for 48 quarters are available, which eases the burden of time series studies as well as cross-sectional analyses. One limitation to using Compustat is that companies' footnote disclosures are not available. Compustat's footnoting system only provides certain supplemental information (e.g., change in accounting method) about data items. Finally, before a tax researcher can adequately use Compustat, a basic level of computer literacy must be obtained. This can be a considerable time investment for tax researchers with a purely legal background. Apart from these weaknesses, Compustat is an excellent data source for some types of studies. It can be the primary data source or simply supplement other data sources.

Other Corporate Databases

Compustat and the Corporate Source Book File are two important computerized sources of corporate data, but they are not the only sources. The National Automated Accounting Research System (NAARS) is also frequently used in tax research. The NAARS data base is offered jointly by Mead Data Central, Inc. and the American Institute of Certified Public Accountants (AICPA) and offers information dating back to 1984 on corporate annual reports to stockholders, governmental unit annual reports, and various accounting literature. A big advantage of using NAARS in tax research is that it includes the full text of corporate financial statements, including notes to financial statements. Most of the *Fortune* ranked companies are included on NAARS, including companies traded on the New York, American, and OTC stock exchanges.

Another data base that can be useful in tax research is the Disclosure Database provided by Disclosure, Inc. in Bethesda, Maryland. This data base provides in-depth financial information on approximately 12,500 companies.[12] Information included in the Disclosure Data base is derived from SEC reports filed by the individual companies and include items such as management's discussion, president's letter on past-year performance, footnotes, significant events, and market conditions relating to the individual company in addition to detailed financial information.

SECTION 2: CORPORATE SOURCE BOOK FILE

Danny P. Hollingsworth
Baylor University

Tax research often requires information contained in corporate tax returns. Unfortunately, this information is confidential for individual firms and researchers

---

[12] This information is contained in *DIALOG Database Catalog* (Palo Alto: Dialog Information Services, Inc., 1991).

must resort to public financial statement disclosures to estimate firms' tax return data. The use of financial statement data in tax research has many weaknesses and is generally inferior to using actual tax return data.[13] The Treasury Department's *Statistics of Income-Corporate Income Tax Returns* [SOI] offers tax researchers a compromise between using financial statement data and individual corporate tax return data. SOI provides detailed, line-item data based on corporate tax returns and reports such data by major and minor industry and by various size categories. A major limitation of SOI is that the data is not firm specific. Therefore, SOI is not an appropriate source if a research project requires firm-level data.

The University of Michigan, Office of Tax Policy Research, maintains a computerized version of the corporate SOI data for each year from 1966 to 1986 on magnetic tape. To obtain information about these computer tapes, contact:

> Joel Slemrod
> The Office of Tax Policy Research
> School of Business Administration
> University of Michigan
> Ann Arbor, MI 48109-1234

Description of Corporate SOI Data

The *Corporation Source Book of Statistics of Income* is published annually and provides the basis for the *SOI, Corporate Income Tax Returns* publication, which is also published annually. Since 1951 the *Corporate Source Book* has been based on information obtained from a stratified probability sample of corporation income tax returns selected after revenue processing, but before audit examination (Washington, 1984, p. 2).

Industry classification used by SOI is based on the Enterprise Standard Industrial Classification (ESIC),[14] which closely follows the Standard Industrial Classification (SIC) (Washington, 1984, p. 2). Table 1 contains a comparison of SIC and ESIC codes with industry groupings used for the 1977 SOI for the mining industry.

The *Corporate Source Book* contains statistics on approximately 60 major industries, depending on the year, and statistics on a number of minor industries within the major industries. In addition, a grouping of major industries into 12 industrial divisions and a U.S. total classification that aggregates all industries are provided.

The *Corporate Source Book* also groups companies by size within a particular industry classification. There are approximately 15 size categories that range from zero assets for the smallest group to assets exceeding $250 million for the largest group. For more recent years, data are combined into fewer size categories (e.g., 12 groups) to avoid reporting data based on too few companies (Washington, 1984, p.

---

[13] The use of financial statement data in tax research has many weaknesses as discussed by Dworin (1985), Fiekowsky (1977), Spooner (1986), and Weiss (1979).

[14] Some variation from the ESIC system is used for the finance industry due to particular IRC provisions (Washington, 1984, p. 2).

TABLE 1
**Comparison of SIC and ESIC Classification with Grouping
Used for Statistics of Income**

SIC	ESIC	SOI
MINING	MINING	MINING
10 Metal Mining	10 Metal Mining	Metal Mining
101 Iron Ores	[No corresponding identification]	1010 Iron Ores
102 Copper Ores		
103 Lead and Zinc Ores	[No corresponding identification]	1070 Copper, lead and zinc, gold and silver ores
104 Gold and Silver Ores		
105 Bauxite and other alum. ores		
106 Ferroalloy, except vanadium	[No corresponding identification]	1098 Other metal mining
108 Metal mining services		
109 Miscellaneous metal ores		
[No corresponding identification]	11 Coal mining	1150 Coal mining
11 Anthracite mining	[No corresponding identification]	
12 Bituminous coal and lignite	[No corresponding identification]	
13 Oil and gas extraction	13 Oil and gas extraction	Oil and gas extraction
131 Crude petr. and natural gas	133 Crude petroleum	1330 Crude petr., natural gas and natural gas liquids
132 Natural gas liquids		
138 Oil and gas field services	138 Oil and gas field services	1380 Oil and gas field services
14 Mining of nonmetallic minerals	14 Nonmetallic minerals	Nonmetallic minerals (except fuels)
141 Dimension stone	[No corresponding identification]	1430 Dimension, crushed, and broken stone, sand and gravel
142 Crushed stone		
144 Sand and gravel		
145 Clay and ceramic minerals		
147 Chemical and fertilizer	[No corresponding identification]	1498 Other nonmetallic minerals
148 Nonmetallic minerals		
149 Miscellaneous nonmetallic		

Source: *A General Description of the Corporation Source Book, 1984*

2). Table 2 lists the breakdowns of the data typically found in the *Corporate Source Book.*.

SOI Data Collection[15]

The corporate SOI data is not merely an aggregation of all corporate tax returns actually filed, but is an estimate, based on stratified probability samples, of all corporate tax returns. The IRS assigns returns to a sampling class or strata as each return is filed and processed (Jamerson, 1991). The criteria used to assign returns to a strata include such characteristics as industry of the company, accounting period used by the company, state of incorporation, and various measures of economic size (e.g., total assets or income) (Jamerson, 1991). Sample returns are selected from each strata based on random numbers associated with each taxpayer's identification number. The probability of a particular return being selected varies greatly, depending on the number and diversity of returns in the stratum and other factors such as whether the stratum is the subject of a special study. However, the method of sample selection is such that a high proportion of returns included in the current year's sample are from taxpayers whose returns were included in earlier samples (Jamerson, 1991).

As with any sampling procedure, the SOI samples contain various errors that researchers should consider. The SOI reports do not directly provide the standard error of the estimate (S_e),[16] but instead provides the coefficient of variation (CV), which can be used to compute the S_e. The S_e is computed by multiplying a sample estimate by its CV. Researchers can use the S_e to construct a confidence interval showing a range of values that should include the actual value 68 percent of the time. Multiplying the S_e by two gives a range of values that should include the actual value 95 percent of the time. These confidence intervals provide researchers information about the entire population of corporate tax returns even though an aggregation of all returns is not provided.

In addition to sampling error, the SOI data may contain taxpayer reporting errors, processing errors, and errors associated with an early cut-off of the sampling process. Missing data from corporate returns included in the sample can also be a source of errors. However, the IRS uses various imputation methods to determine estimates for the missing data. Data quality is maintained by subjecting the corporate returns to numerous quality control measures (e.g., 100 percent key verification, independent reprocessing of certain statistically processed returns, and analysis of various data combinations). Finally, many SOI tables have values with asterisks (*) indicating the data may be unreliable because it is based on a very small (i.e., less than ten) set of observations.

Information on sample design and data limitations is found in each SOI report, including appropriate references. Also, the Director of the SOI Division of the IRS[17] can provide additional information about the sampling procedure.

---

[15] The discussion in this section came from information compiled by Bettye Jamerson, *SOI Bulletin* (Summer 1991), Appendix A, p. 143.

[16] Standard error of the estimate (S_e) is an index used to determine the magnitude of error arising from the use of predictions based on sample data to estimate actual data items. See Shavelson (1981, p. 242) for a further discussion of the S_e.

[17] P. O. Box 2608, Washington, D.C. 20013-2608

TABLE 2
Data Found in the Corporate Source Book

Industry

Major or minor industry code (e.g., 1150 = coal mining)

Year

Income tax returns with accounting period ended July 19XX through June 19XX
(e.g. 1988 source book would be July 1988 through June 1989).

Size of Total Assets (in $1,000)

Zero Assets		
1 — under 100	5,000 — under 10,000	250,000 or more
100 — under 250	10,000 — under 25,000	
250 — under 500	25,000 — under 50,000	
500 — under 1,000	50,000 — under 100,000	
1,000 — under 5,000	100,000 — under 250,000	

Data Items

1.	Number of Returns	32.	Less Cost of Treasury Stock
2.	Total Assets	33.	Total Receipts
3.	Cash	34.	Business Receipts
4.	Notes and Accounts Receivable	35.	Interest
5.	Less Allowance for Bad Debts		Interest on Govt Obligations:
6.	Inventories	36.	State and Local
	Investments in Govt. Obligations:	37.	Rents
7.	Total	38.	Royalties
8.	Other Current Assets	39.	Net S-T Cap Gain Less Net LT Loss
9.	Loans to Stockholders	40.	Net L-T Cap Gain Less Net ST Loss
10.	Mortgage and Real Estate Loans	41.	Net Gain, Noncapital Assets
11.	Other Investments	42.	Dividends, Domestic Corporations
12.	Depreciable Assets	43.	Dividends, Foreign Corporations
13.	Less: Accumulated Depreciation	44.	Other Receipts
14.	Depletable Assets	45.	Total Deductions
15.	Less: Accumulated Depletion	46.	Cost of Sales and Operations
16.	Land	47.	Compensation of Officers
17.	Intangible Assets (Amortizable)	48.	Repairs
18.	Less: Accumulated Amortization	49.	Bad Debts
19.	Other Assets	50.	Rent Paid On Business Property
20.	Total Liabilities	51.	Taxes Paid
21.	Accounts Payable	52.	Interest Paid
22.	Mort, Notes, and Bonds under 1 Yr.	53.	Contributions or Gifts
23.	Other Current Liabilities	54.	Amortization
24.	Loans From Stockholders	55.	Depreciation
25.	Mort, Notes, Bonds, 1 Yr. or More	56.	Depletion
26.	Other Liabilities	57.	Advertising
27.	Capital Stock	58.	Pension, Prof Sh, Stock, Annuity
28.	Paid-in or Capital Surplus	59.	Employee Benefit Programs
29.	Retained Earnings, Appropriated	60.	Net Loss, Noncapital Assets
30.	Retained Earnings, Unappropriated	61.	Other Deductions
31.	Other Retained Earnings (1120S)	62.	Total Receipts Less Total Deducts

TABLE 2 (Continued)

63. Const Taxable Inc Frm Rel Frn Corps	75. Inc Tax (Before Cred), Total (Tx)
64. Net Income (Less Deficit), Total	76. Regular Tax (Tax II)
65. Net Income Total	77. Personal Holding Company Tax
66. Deficit, Total	78. Recapture of Investment Credit
67. Net income (Less Def) Form 1120-A	79. Alternative Minimum Tax
68. Net income (Less Def) Form 1120S	80. Environmental Tax
69. Net income (Less Def), 1120F	81. Foreign Tax Credit
70. Statutory Special Deductions, Total	82. U.S. Possessions Tax Credit
71. Net Operating Loss Deduction	83. Orphan Drug Credit
72. Dividends Received Deduction	84. Nonconventional Source Fuel Credit
73. Public Utility Div Paid Deduction	85. General Business Credit
74. Income Subject To Tax	86. Prior Year Minimum Tax Credit

Data Items Available For Other Years

Investment Tax Credit	Invest Credit: Cost of Property
Nonrefundable Energy Credit	Investment Qualified for Credit
Travel, Entertainment & Gift Expense	Tentative Credit
Distributions to Stockholders:	Credit Carryover
Cash and Property	Energy Invest Credit: Cost of Prop.
Corporation's Own Stock	Investment Qualified For Credit
	Total Tax Preference Items
	Disc Export Gross Receipts

Source: *Source Book Statistics of Income 1988, Corporation Income Tax Returns*

Use of Corporate SOI Data in Tax Research

A variety of research studies have used corporate SOI data, either as a primary data source or to supplement other data. In addition, SOI data has been used to verify the reasonableness of data obtained elsewhere (e.g., financial statements). The following research studies are not exhaustive of studies using corporate SOI data, but they do provide examples of how such data can be useful.

Pasurka (1984) used the Treasury Department's *SOI-1972, Corporation Income Tax Returns* to investigate the impact that the U.S. corporate income tax has on the competitiveness of the U.S. in international trade. The U.S. corporate income tax is a direct tax rather than an indirect tax, and thus it is not eligible for border tax adjustments. Since most European countries have value-added taxes, which are indirect taxes, their exports to the U.S. receive border tax adjustments. A question arises as to whether the reliance of the U.S. on direct taxes such as the corporate income tax places it at a competitive disadvantage with European countries. The *SOI-1972, Corporate Income Tax Returns* publication was the source for obtaining receipts, cost of sales, net income, tax and credit items, distributions to stockholders, total assets, net worth, depreciable assets and depreciation deduction by minor industry. This information was used to compute corporate tax paid by industry. The results of Pasurka's study indicate that corporate income taxes have an adverse impact on the level of protection given U.S. firms.

Morgan and Mutti (1985) studied the exportation of state and local taxes to residents of other states. In their study Morgan and Mutti used several data services, one of which was the Treasury Department's *SOI-1980, Corporation Income Tax Returns* publication, to determine the extent that state corporate income taxes and property taxes are exported to other states through shifting the taxes forward to consumers, shifting taxes backwards to labor or investors, or reduction in federal tax liabilities. The Treasury's SOI was used to obtain data on net income, interest paid and rent paid by corporations. The results indicate that considerable differences exist among the states regarding the exportation of business taxes.

Swenson (1987) also used the U.S. Treasury's *SOI-1980, Corporation Income Tax Returns* publication to gather data to test the neutrality and equity aspects of the Accelerated Cost Recovery System (ACRS). This study analyzed how the effect of inflation on corporate taxation was affected by ACRS, and whether the effect was consistent across industries. Using Monte Carlo simulation over a projected 20-year period, Swenson analyzed 38 industries in testing whether the use of ACRS during inflationary periods resulted in neutrality for the tax system as a whole and as well as among industries. The results show that when inflation is between 9 and 13 percent, ACRS depreciation is equivalent to general price-level adjusted depreciation (i.e., inflation-neutral). With respect to neutrality across industries, Swenson found that ACRS corrects for under-depreciation in some industries, but over compensates for under-depreciation in capital intensive industries.

Omer and Reiter (1991) used pension funding levels of firms in different industries to study the role that tax incentives have on business decisions. A sample of 408 firms was selected from companies contained on the *FASB 36 data tape, Compustat data file,* and *The Blue Book of Pension Funds.* In addition to these data sources, the Treasury Department's *SOI, Corporate Tax Returns*[18] was used to capture dimensions of tax motivation (e.g., tax depreciation, credits, income subject to tax) that influence pension funding. Specifically, four tax incentive ratios were used to determine which major industry groups are more likely to engage in a pension overfunding strategy.

The ratio of pension expense to gross margin was used as a proxy for flexibility—the ability of a firm to alter its tax saving strategy in the short-run. Depreciation expense to gross margin and net taxes after credits to income subject to tax were used as proxies for vulnerability, which represents the degree to which firms risk losing the use of tax benefits by choosing a pension funding tax saving strategy. As a proxy for tax benefits, Omer and Reiter use total taxes to income subject to taxes. This ratio measures the degree that firms are motivated to engage in tax savings activities (i.e., pension overfunding).

The results show that 14 of the 408 sample companies were "likely" to engage in pension overfunding, 62 were classified as "unlikely," and 332 as "other," which includes companies that do not clearly fit in either the "likely" or the "unlikely" category. In comparing the actual pension funding status with the above classifica-

---

[18] Omer and Reiter actually used the Corporate Source Book tape from the University of Michigan instead of the hard bound version issued by the Treasury Department.

tions, Omer and Reiter found that "likely" firms have higher funding levels and "unlikely" firms have lower levels of funding.

Data Limitations and Concluding Remarks on The Corporate Source Book File

The SOI, Corporate Tax Return publications (including the University of Michigan's magnetic tapes) are very useful for certain tax research projects. There are limitations with the SOI data, however, that restrict its usefulness in some cases. First, the data is aggregated based on stratified probability sampling procedures. Thus, research projects seeking data on individual companies could not use the SOI as a data source. For example, data for banks in the Northeast with assets exceeding $1 billion could not be obtained from SOI. A second limitation relates to comparability of data over a period of years. SOI data is affected by consolidations, mergers, changes in tax law, changes in tax forms, and industry classification systems (Washington, 1984).

The third limitation arises when using SOI data in conjunction with data from other sources such as Compustat. Matching SOI's industry classification with individual SIC codes for particular companies can be difficult. SOI classifies companies according to the industry in which it has the largest percentage of receipts (Washington, 1984). Thus, large diversified corporations will be included in only one industry even though it may have operations in a variety of industries. A final limitation relates to data availability. As with most data sources, certain data required for some research projects is not available from SOI. Swenson (1987) had such a problem in analyzing the relationship between ACRS depreciation and inflation. In this study, Swenson was required to make assumptions such as the tax-accounting lives of industries' fixed assets because such information was not available.

In conclusion, the Treasury Department's *SOI, Corporate Income Tax Returns* publications and the University of Michigan's magnetic tapes are an excellent source of tax return data. In fact, this is essentially the only source of corporate tax return data that is publicly available to all researchers. The tapes maintained by the University of Michigan make time-series studies or cross-sectional studies across industries easier and more efficient than would otherwise be possible. There are trade-offs such as the cost of obtaining data[19] and limitations of the data that must be carefully evaluated before using the SOI as a source of data for tax research.

---

[19] The Corporate Annual Source Book file costs about $600 per year and the Combined Corporate file that contains years 1966 through 1987 costs about $2,000.

Appendix A
Sample Program for Creating Subsamples Directly from The Compustat Tapes

```
DATA SUBSAMP.DAT (DROP=I J COL YR);
ARRAY V{350};
  INFILE CMPUSTAT;
  DO YR = 1 TO 20;
    INPUT #1
        @9 DNUM RB4.
        @13 CNUM $CHAR8.
        @21 CIC RB4.
        @25 REC RB4.
        @29 FILE RB4.
        @33 ZLIST RB4.
        @37 INAME $CHAR28.
        @65 CONAME $CHAR28.
        @93 SMBL $CHAR8.@;
    COL = 101 + (4*(YR-1));
    INPUT #1
        @COL (FYR YEAR) (RB4. + 76) @;
    INPUT #1
        @261
        (XREL STK DUP) (RB4.)@;
    COL = 333 + (4*(YR-1));
    INPUT #1
        @COL CODE RB4.@;
    COL = 1113 + 700*YR;
    DO I = 1 TO 175;
        INPUT #1 @COL V{I} RB4.@;
        V{I} = ROUND (V{I},.0001);
        IF V{I} = .0001 THEN V{I} = .;
        COL = COL + 4;
    END;
    INPUT #2
        @33 STATE RB4.
        @37 COUNTY RB4.
        @41 FINC RB4.@;
    COL = 45 + 4*(YR-1);
    INPUT #2
        @COL SOURCE RB4.@;
    INPUT #2
        @137 EIN $CHAR12.@;
    COL = 1113 + (700*YR);
    DO J = 176 TO 350;
        INPUT #2 @COL V{J} RB4.@;
        V{J} = ROUND(V{J},.0001);
        IF V{J} = .0001 THEN V{J} = .;
        COL = COL + 4;
    END;
    KEEP XXX XXX XXX;
    IF YEAR GE XX AND YR LE XX THEN OUTPUT;
    END;
```

Appendix B
Sample Program for Creating Permanent SAS Data Sets from the Compustat Tapes

```
DATA ANNUAL.XXX (DROP=I J COL YR COMPRESS=YES);
ARRAY V{350};
  INFILE CMPUSTAT;
  DO YR = 1 TO 20;
    INPUT #1
      @9 DNUM RB4.
      @13 CNUM $CHAR8.
      @21 CIC RB4.
      @25 REC RB4.
      @29 FILE RB4.
      @33 ZLIST RB4.
      @37 INAME $CHAR28.
      @65 CONAME $CHAR28.
      @93 SMBL $CHAR8.@;
    COL = 101 + (4*(YR-1));
    INPUT #1
      @COL (FYR YEAR) (RB4. + 76) @;
    INPUT #1
      @261
      (XREL STK DUP) (RB4.)@;
    COL = 333 + (4*(YR-1));
    INPUT #1
      @COL CODE RB4.@;
    COL = 1113 + 700*YR;
    DO I = 1 TO 175;
      INPUT #1 @COL V{I} RB4.@;
      V{I} = ROUND (V{I},.0001);
      IF V{I} = .0001 THEN V{I} = .;
      COL = COL + 4;
    END;
    INPUT #2
      @33 STATE RB4.
      @37 COUNTY RB4.
      @41 FINC RB4.@;
    COL = 45 + 4*(YR-1);
    INPUT #2
      @COL SOURCE RB4.@;
    INPUT #2
      @137 EIN $CHAR12.@;
    COL = 1113 + (700*YR);
    DO J = 176 TO 350;
      INPUT #2 @COL V{J} RB4.@;
      V{J} = ROUND(V{J},.0001);
      IF V{J} = .0001 THEN V{J} = .;
      COL = COL + 4;
    END;
    IF YEAR > 0 AND YR < 21 THEN OUTPUT;
    END;
```

Appendix C
Program for Creating Subsamples of Permanent SAS Data Sets

THIS PROGRAM CREATES A PERMANENT SAS DATA SET CALLED
"ANNUAL.SUBSAMPL" THAT IS A SUBSET OF ONE OF THE COMPUSTAT
DATA SETS. THE SUBSETS ARE CREATED BY USING ONE OR MORE OF THE
"WHERE" STATEMENTS.

NOTE: IF USING MORE THAN ONE WHERE STATEMENT, CHANGE
"WHERE" TO "WHERE SAME AND" FOR ALL WHERE STATEMENTS
AFTER THE FIRST ONE.

TO USE, REPLACE ANNUAL.**** WITH THE REFERENCE TO THE APPROPRIATE
DATA SET. FOR EXAMPLE, IF YOU WISH TO ACCESS THE OVER-THE-
COUNTER FILE, CHANGE "SET ANNUAL.*****" TO "SET ANNUAL.OTCR"   ;

DATA SASDAT.SUBSAMPL;
  SET ANNUAL.****;

THE FOLLOWING WHERE STATEMENTS SUBSET DATA BY KEEPING ONLY
SELECTED FIRMS

TO USE, REMOVE "*" FROM APPROPRIATE "WHERE" STATEMENT AND FILL
IN CNUMS OF FIRMS THAT WANT TO INCLUDE IN SAMPLE

NOTE: EXPAND CNUM LIST IF NECESSARY   ;

```
*       WHERE CNUM EQ '449842' OR CNUM EQ '755078';
*       WHERE CNUM BETWEEN '000001' AND '002000';
```

THE FOLLOWING WHERE STATEMENTS SUBSET DATA BY KEEPING ONLY FIRMS
IN SELECTED INDUSTRIES

TO USE, REMOVE "*" FROM APPROPRIATE "WHERE" STATEMENT AND FILL IN
DNUMS OF INDUSTRIES WANT TO INCLUDE IN SAMPLE

NOTE: EXPAND DNUM LIST IF NECESSARY   ;

```
*       WHERE DNUM EQ 0800 OR DNUM EQ 1000;
*       WHERE DNUM BETWEEN 0200 AND 1040;
```

THE FOLLOWING WHERE STATEMENTS SUBSET DATA BY KEEPING ONLY DATA
FROM SELECTED YEARS.

TO USE, REMOVE "*" FROM APPROPRIATE "WHERE" STATEMENT AND FILL IN
YEARS WANT TO INCLUDE IN SAMPLE

NOTE: EXPAND YEAR LIST IF NECESSARY   ;

```
*       WHERE YEAR EQ 79 OR YEAR EQ 83;
*       WHERE YEAR BETWEEN 86 AND 90;
```

THE FOLLOWING WHERE STATEMENTS SUBSETS DATA BY KEEPING ONLY
    SELECTED VARIABLES

TO USE, REMOVE "*" BEFORE "KEEP" AND FILL IN VARIABLES WANT TO
    INCLUDE IN SAMPLE   ;

*   **KEEP CNUM YEAR V1-V12;**

THE FOLLOWING STATEMENTS CREATE LAGGED DATA VALUES.
TO USE, REMOVE "*" FROM THE FOLLOWING STATEMENTS AND CHANGE VXXX
    AND VXXXL1 TO THE DESIRED VARIABLE (EX. CHANGE TO V1 OR V102)

      NOTES:
              1) TO LAG MORE THAN ONE VARIABLE, DUPLICATE THE LAST TWO
                  STATEMENTS AS MANY TIMES AS NECESSARY.

              2) TO LAG A VARIABLE FOR MORE THAN ONE PERIOD, CREATE THE
                  FOLLOWING STATEMENTS:
                  CNUML2 = LAG2(CNUM);
                  VXXXL2 = LAG2(VXXX);
                    IF CNUML2 NE CNUM THEN VXXXL2 = .;   ;

*   **CNUML1 = LAG1 (CNUM);**
*   **VXXXL1 = LAG1 (VXXX);**
*   **IF CNUML1 NE CNUM THEN VXXXL1 = .;**

THE FOLLOWING PROC CREATES A NEW PERMANENT SAS DATA SET THAT
    CONTAINS NO FIRMS WITH MISSING VALUES FOR SPECIFIED VARIABLES

TO USE, REMOVE THE "/*" BEFORE PROC SQL, REMOVE THE "*/" AT THE
END OF THE PROGRAM, AND CHANGE THE VARIABLE LIST AS NECESSARY.

NOTE: EXPAND OR REDUCE VARIABLE LIST AS NEEDED   ;

```
/* PROC SQL;
      CREATE TABLE SASDAT.NOMISS AS
         SELECT * FROM SASDAT.SUBSAMPL
            WHERE CNUM NOT IN
                (SELECT DISTINCT CNUM FROM SASDAT.SUBSAMPL
                    WHERE  (V1  IS MISSING OR
                            V2  IS MISSING OR
                            V3  IS MISSING OR
                            V4  IS MISSING OR
                            V5  IS MISSING OR
                            V6  IS MISSING OR
                            V7  IS MISSING OR
                            V8  IS MISSING OR
                            V9  IS MISSING OR
                            V10 IS MISSING OR
                            V11 IS MISSING OR
                            V12 IS MISSING)); */
```

REFERENCES

Bernard, V., and C. Hayn. 1986. Inflation and the Distribution of the Corporate Income Tax Burden. *National Tax Journal* (June): 172-187.

Bodie, Z., J. O. Light, R. Morck, and R. A. Taggart, Jr. 1984. Funding and Asset Allocation in Corporate Pension Plans: An Empirical Investigation. Working Paper 1315, National Bureau of Economic Research, Cambridge, MA.

Bruttomesso, R. I., and J. E. Ketz. 1982. Historical Cost and General Price Level Tax Rates in Seven Industries. *The Journal of the American Taxation Association* (Winter): 30-44.

Crum, R. P. 1985. Value-Added Tax Collection Alternatives: Their Revenue, Cash Flow, and Micro Tax Policy Effects. *The Journal of the American Taxation Association* (Fall): 52-72.

————. 1991. Financing Value-Added Tax Cash Flows. *The Journal of the American Taxation Association* (Spring): 1-35.

Davidson, S., and R. L. Weil. 1975. Inflation Accounting: What Will General Price Level Adjusted Income Statements Show. *Financial Analysts Journal* (January-February): 27-31, 71-84.

Dworin, L. 1985. On Estimating Corporate Tax Liabilities from Financial Statements. *Tax Notes* (December 2): 965-971.

Eisner, Robert, Steven H. Albert, and Martin A. Sullivan. 1984. The New Incremental Tax Credit for R&D: Incentive or Disincentive. *The National Tax Journal* (June): 171-183.

Fiekowsky, S. 1977. Pitfalls in the Computation of Effective Tax Rates Paid by Corporations. U.S. Treasury Department, Office of Tax Analysis (July).

Francis, J. R., and S. A. Reiter. 1987. Determinants of Corporate Pension Funding Strategy. *Journal of Accounting and Economics* 9 (April): 35-60.

Friedman, B. F. 1982. Pension Funding, Pension Asset Allocation, and Corporate Finance: Evidence from Individual Company Data. Working Paper 957, National Bureau of Economic Research, Cambridge, MA.

Halperin, Robert M., and William N. Lanen. 1987. The Effects of the *Thor Power Tool* Decision on the LIFO/FIFO Choice. *The Accounting Review* (April): 378-384.

Jamerson, B. 1991. General Description of Statistics of Income Sample Procedures and Data Limitations. *SOI Bulletin* (Summer): 143-145.

Morgan, W. E., and J. H. Mutti. 1985. The Exportation of State and Local Taxes in a Multilateral Framework: The Case of Business Type Taxes. *National Tax Journal* (June): 191-208.

Omer, T. C., K. H. Molloy, and D. A. Ziebart. 1991. Measurement of Effective Corporate Tax Rates Using Financial Statement Information. *The Journal of the American Taxation Association* (Spring): 57-72.

————, and S. A. Reiter. 1991. Measuring Tax Incentives. Working Paper, University of Illinois, Champaign, IL.

Parker, J. E. 1977. Impact of Price Level Accounting. *The Accounting Review* (January): 69-96.

Pasurka, C. A. 1984. Corporate Income Taxes and U.S. Effective Rates of Protection. *National Tax Journal* (December): 529-537.

Schmidt, Dennis R. 1986. Apportionment of Multijurisdictional Corporate Income. *The Journal of the American Taxation Association* (Fall): 19-34.

Shavelson, R. J. 1981. *Statistical Reasoning for the Behavioral Sciences*. Boston: Allyn and Bacon, Inc.

Shevlin, T. 1987. Taxes and Off-Balance-Sheet Financing: Research and Development Limited Partnerships. *The Accounting Review* (July): 480-509.

————. 1990. Estimating Corporate Marginal Tax Rates with Asymmetric Tax Treatment of Gains and Losses. *The Journal of the American Taxation Association* (Spring): 51-67.

————, and S. Porter. 1992. The Corporate Tax Comeback in 1987: Some Further Evidence. *The Journal of the American Taxation Association* (Spring): 58-79.

Spooner, G. M. 1986. Effective Tax Rates from Financial Statements. *National Tax Journal* (September): 293-306.

Swenson, C. W. 1987. An Analysis of ACRS During Inflationary Periods. *The Accounting Review* (January): 117-136.

Thomas, Jacob K. 1988. Corporate Taxes and Defined Benefit Pension Plans. *Journal of Accounting and Economics* (July): 199-237.

Washington, J. C. 1984. Corporation Source Book of Statistics of Income. *A General Description of the Corporation Source Book*, Publication 647, Department of Treasury.

Weiss, R. 1979. Effective Corporation Income Tax Rates. *National Tax Journal* (September): 380-389.

Wilkie, Patrick J. 1988. Corporate Average Effective Tax Rates and Inferences About Relative Tax Preference. *The Journal of the American Taxation Association* (Fall): 75-88.

Zimmerman, J. L. 1983. Taxes and Firm Size. *Journal of Accounting and Economics* (August): 119-149.

Chapter 4
Canadian Income Tax Data

Alan Macnaughton
University of Waterloo

Introduction

Many countries have constructed personal and corporate income tax models based on samples of tax returns, but generally only the aggregate statistics produced by such microsimulation models have been made publicly available (Lietmeyer 1986; OECD 1988). Access to the actual microdata and model is much more helpful since it allows users to perform their own simulations and statistical analyses. Until recently the United States has been the only country to provide access to tax microdata, in the form of the Individual Tax Model Files and the Statistics of Income Panel of Individual Returns.[1] Neither data set has an associated microsimulation model to recalculate tax liabilities under proposed changes to tax rules.[2] In 1988, Canada jointly released a body of tax microdata and an associated microsimulation model—Statistics Canada's Social Policy Simulation Database and Model (SPSD/M).[3]

This article examines the SPSD/M and describes its potential uses for academic tax research. American researchers should find the SPSD/M interesting not only because Canada and the United States have similar economies and tax structures, but also because its data is in some respects richer than the U.S. Individual Tax Model Files and therefore allows examination of a wider range of hypotheses. Since the SPSD/M is quite new and is based on state-of-the-art statistical, economic and computer methodologies, it may also be interesting to researchers wishing to improve the methodological underpinnings of microsimulation models.[4]

---

[1] The Swedish and Norwegian governments allow outside users to submit SAS jobs to run on their microdata files of personal tax returns, although the output of each run is examined closely for violations of personal privacy restrictions prior to release. For further information, write to Mr. Ingemar Eriksson, Ministry of Finance Economic Dept., S-103 33, Stockholm, Sweden.

[2] Although users can construct their own microsimulation model, this can involve considerable expense and can lead to wasteful duplication of effort among different users.

[3] Microdata files containing fewer tax variables are available for several other countries (Sutherland 1991). For example, in the U.K., statutory tax rules have been applied to Family Expenditure Survey microdata to create TAXMOD (Atkinson and Sutherland 1988). Also, the Luxembourg Income Study Database (Smeeding et al. 1988) provides data on the same or similar variables for ten countries. It includes many demographic and income-source variables, but only one explicit income-tax variable—the amount payable.

[4] For example, computer scientists Cotton and Sadowsky (1989) have compared the computing environment of the SPSD/M to that of the TRIM2 model produced by the Urban Institute in the U.S. Based on this comparison, they provide a number of recommendations for improving both models.

Acknowledgements: I would like to thank Charles Enis of Penn State University, Glenn Feltham and Suzanne Paquette of the University of Waterloo, and especially Brian Murphy of Statistics Canada's SPSD/M project team for helpful comments on earlier drafts of this paper.

The article also reviews other sources of Canadian personal and corporate tax data.

General Description of the SPSD/M

The purpose of the SPSD/M is to facilitate the analysis of social policy by enabling an assessment of the cost implications and income redistributive effects of changes in the personal income tax and cash transfer systems at both the federal and provincial levels of government. The SPSD/M contains enough information to calculate both personal income tax payable and cash transfers received for all individuals in the sample. The current version of the SPSD/M, which is numbered 4.1, is primarily based on 1986 data. A new version is expected to be issued every two years; version 5.0, which is to be released sometime in 1992, is based on 1988 data. Each version of the SPSD/M released so far has been a cross-section for a single year, like the U.S. Individual Tax Model Files (Enis 1991). At present there does not exist any multi-year data like the Statistics of Income Panel of Individual Returns (Crum 1991; Flesher undated).[5]

The SPSD/M includes: a database of information for each individual and household in the sample; a set of algorithms for computing personal income tax and cash transfers; data retrieval and reporting software which is used to set up simulations and report their results; and a comprehensive set of manuals, containing fully-worked examples, which explain its use.[6]

The educational price for the SPSD/M is $3,000 for a single copy and $7,500 for a site licence. In order to obtain the educational price, the SPSD/M must not be used for earning consulting fees or research grant stipends. The non-educational price is $5,000 for one copy and $12,500 for a site licence. When version 5.0 becomes available, it will have to be purchased separately; no discount will be provided to purchasers of previous versions, although any updates issued before the next version is released will be provided free. On the release of version 5.0, users planning to use the SPSD/M for teaching purposes only will be able to purchase version 4.1 for only $1,500.

Unlike the mainframe-based U.S. Individual Tax Model Files, the SPSD/M is designed to be run on a DOS-based (IBM-compatible) microcomputer. The minimum hardware requirements are an IBM PC with 512 kilobytes of memory (640 kilobytes preferred), a high density floppy drive, and a hard disk with 10 megabytes of free space. The SPSD/M team estimates that a simulation run takes approximately 3 minutes with a 486-model microcomputer, 10 minutes with a 386/25 model and 55 minutes with a 286 model. A math co-processor is highly recommended; without one, these estimated run times would be increased by roughly a factor of 10.

---

[5] Statistics Canada is now well into the planning stages of a new Survey of Labour and Income Dynamics which, when complete, will be a source of longitudinal microdata. The imputation of tax data onto this file is being considered but public release is at least five years away.

[6] Other short descriptions of the SPSD/M are Wolfson et al. (1989) and Bordt et al. (1990). For more information, phone (613) 951-3774 or write to: Social and Economic Studies Division, Analytical Studies Branch, Statistics Canada, R. H. Coats Building, Tunney's Pasture, Ottawa, Canada K1A 0T6.

One advantage of the SPSD/M relative to the U.S. Individual Tax Model Files is that in the SPSD/M the family relationships within each household in the sample are known. This information is required for some tax calculations such as tax credits for dependants. More importantly, though, it allows the analyst considerable freedom in choosing an appropriate unit of analysis for assessing the distributional consequences of tax changes. Many researchers consider that the family rather than the individual is the appropriate unit for distributional analyses because income and consumption goods may be shared within the family. Five different units of analysis are supported by the SPSD/M:

- individual—a single person or record;
- nuclear family—a head, a spouse if present, and never-married children under the age of 18 sharing the same dwelling;
- census family—differs from a nuclear family in that there is no age restriction on the children;
- economic family—a group of individuals living together who are all related by blood, marriage or adoption and share the same dwelling; and
- household—all individuals sharing the same dwelling.

Each variable in the SPSD/M is stored at either the individual or household level. For example, age and employment income are individual-level variables while province and shelter expenditures are household-level variables.

The second advantage of the SPSD/M is that it provides a broader set of variables than the U.S. Individual Tax Model Files. As Luttman (1990) notes, personal income tax databases generally do not include the demographic and social-science variables needed for many empirical research projects. One of these variables included in the SPSD/M is labour supply (number of weeks worked). A complete list of the variables included in the database is given below.

1. Demographic: age, sex, province, size of urban area, years since immigration, marital status (including common-law), and disability status.
2. Education: highest educational level achieved, educational status (student/nonstudent), and school type currently attending.
3. Family Structure: 72 variables which place each individual in his or her family context, such as relationship to head of household, number of children in household, number of elderly in household, etc.
4. Income Receipts: earnings from employment, farming net income, benefits received from the Canada/Quebec Pension Plan (a government-run contributory pension plan), non-farming self-employment net income, net income from roomers and boarders, other taxable income, non-taxable money income, interest income, dividend income from Canadian corporations, other investment income, and pension income.
5. Labour Force: industry, occupation, labour force status, weeks worked, last year full/part time, weeks unemployed, number of stretches unemployed last year, major non-labour-force activity, and several other variables relating to Unemployment Insurance claims.

6. Housing Characteristics: tenure (i.e., owning or renting), number of rooms, number of bedrooms, market value of home, and mortgage outstanding on home.

7. Income-Tax-Specific Variables: capital gains, expenses deductible from employment income, carrying charges, union and professional dues, other deductions (e.g., moving expenses and alimony), child care expense deduction, business investment losses (i.e., losses on disposition of shares or debt of small businesses), contributions to registered pension plans (i.e., private pension plans), contributions to RRSPs (similar to U.S. IRAs), capital loss carryover deduction, non-capital loss carryover deduction, tax credits for dependants other than spouse and children, charitable donations, disability tax credit, education tax credit, medical expense tax credit, foreign tax credit applied against surtax, investment tax credit, federal political contribution tax credit, other federal tax credits (e.g., foreign tax credit), tuition fees, and the total of selected provincial tax credits.

8. Expenditure Patterns: amounts spent on 40 expenditure categories (chosen to exactly match input-output table categories), interest on personal loans, other money receipts (e.g., inheritances), sale of durables, saving or dissaving in year, income taxes paid, property taxes, and mortgage interest paid.

The SPSD/M calculates a number of other tax and transfer amounts by applying the statutory rules to the above data.[7] Regarding transfer programs, the main calculations are amounts received from the Canada/Quebec Pension Plan, Old Age Security and Guaranteed Income Supplement (respectively, universal and means-tested benefits to seniors), Unemployment Insurance benefits, Social Assistance (welfare payments), and Family Allowance (Canada's system of monthly payments to parents of dependant children). The chief personal income tax calculations are: surtax, tax credits for dependants, age tax credit, child tax credit, required contributions to Unemployment Insurance and the Canada/Quebec Pension Plan, alternative minimum tax, capital gains deduction, dividend tax credit, pension income tax credit, the "clawback" of family allowances and Old Age Security payments for high-income individuals, and various provincial tax credits. Of course, the SPSD/M also calculates net income for tax purposes, taxable income, and federal and provincial income tax payable.

The income tax calculation algorithm in the SPSD/M uses many variables other than the income-tax-specific variables listed in item 7 above. For example, most of the information on sources of income is taken from the income-receipts variables listed in item 4 above and the transfer payments mentioned earlier.

A useful byproduct of the SPSD/M tax calculation is the marginal income tax rate. This is quite comprehensive since it includes both federal and provincial

---

[7] Although the SPSD/M manuals explain these calculations in some detail, researchers who are unfamiliar with Canadian tax rules may wish to consult a Canadian tax text such as Beam and Laiken (1991). For other Canadian references, see a teaching handout available from the author entitled "Legal Research in Tax: UW and WLU Library Resources."

taxes—cities and other sub-provincial levels of government in Canada do not impose income taxes.[8]

Another algorithm in the SPSD/M estimates the amounts of federal and provincial commodity taxes paid. The federal commodity taxes include Goods and Services Tax (value-added tax), custom import duties, alcohol and tobacco excise taxes and excise duties, gasoline excise tax, and energy-use taxes. Provincial commodity taxes include retail sales tax, gasoline tax, amusement tax, and liquor taxes. An important characteristic of these taxes is the cascading effect which occurs when a tax rate is applied to the value of a commodity inclusive of another tax type. The total burden of these taxes on consumers is estimated by using an input-output model. Thus, the SPSD/M provides for each individual an estimate of the amount paid for each of these commodity taxes. The total amount of these taxes is also allocated by 40 expenditure categories. A future version of the SPSD/M will include an input/output modelling language that allows the user to recalculate these amounts using different parameters.

Construction of the SPSD/M

The SPSD/M is not a conventional database. It is important to understand the construction of the SPSD/M in some detail in order to understand the uses to which it can legitimately be put.[9]

Since no single database contains all of the variables listed above, the SPSD/M has been created by merging information from four different databases: Statistics Canada's Survey of Consumer Finance/Labour Force Survey (SCF), Revenue Canada's "Green Book" file of personal tax returns, Employment and Immigration Canada's microdata file of Unemployment Insurance claim histories, and Statistics Canada's Family Expenditure Survey. The SCF provides mostly the demographic, education, family structure and income receipts variables. However, as high-income individuals are under-represented on the SCF, the income-receipts data for individuals with incomes above $80,000 is instead taken from the Green Book file. The sample sizes of these databases are large: 70,000 individuals for the SCF; 300,000 individuals for the Green Book file; 30,000 individuals for the Unemployment Insurance data; and 10,000 households for the Family Expenditure survey.

A direct linkage of these four databases—that is, matching identical individuals across the data sources—is undesirable from the point of view of protecting individuals' privacy. Also, because few individuals are on all four databases, it would greatly shrink the size of the sample. Therefore, the SPSD/M is constructed using a series of statistical-matching techniques which link similar individuals in the four databases to form a single internally consistent and statistically representative database of synthetic individuals. In other words, the variables given for a single individual in the SPSD/M were not actually observed for one person, but rather for

---

[8] These governments rely instead on the property tax. The amount of property tax paid is one of the expenditure-pattern variables included in the SPSD/M.

[9] For more details, see Wolfson et al. (1987) and Statistics Canada (1987).

at least four different, but statistically similar, persons in the four component databases.

In constructing the SPSD/M, the initial or "host" database is the SCF, while the other databases are the "donors." The main statistical-matching technique used for this data-donation process is called "categorical matching" in the SPSD/M documentation and "hot deck matching method involving the use of ranks" in the statistical literature (Armstrong 1989, Singh et al. 1990).[10] In this technique, classification variables such as age, province and sex are used to partition the host and donor databases into identically-defined "bins" of records, which are then sorted based on one of the common variables (e.g., total income). This matching variable is then used to pair records in a given bin one-for-one across the two databases (i.e., record n of bin m of database A is matched with record n of bin m in database B). If a one-for-one pairing is not possible because the bins for the two databases initially contain an unequal number of records, then records are duplicated or deleted as required.[11]

The categorical matching technique was used to merge each of the following donor databases with the SCF: the Unemployment Insurance database, the Family Expenditure database, and the income-receipts data (item 4 above) taken from the Green Book file for higher-income individuals. The merging of income-receipts data from the Green Book file involved one additional complication: to protect privacy, data on specific individuals was not used directly. Instead, prior to categorical matching, the Green Book records were cross-classified by groupings of age, employment income, investment income, dividend income and capital gains, and then a weighted average of the variables was taken. As a result of this micro-record aggregation technique, each income number used is a weighted average of at least 5 similar individuals.[12]

A different statistical-matching technique called stochastic imputation was used for the remainder of the Green Book data (item 7 above). The first step was to use variables which are common to both the SCF and Green Book databases to partition the records in both databases into identically-defined bins.[13] Next, the statistical distribution of each of the tax variables was estimated separately for each

---

[10] The term "hot deck" comes from a class of methods of imputation for item non-response in which "the value assigned for a missing response is taken from a respondent to the current survey" (Kalton and Kasprzyk 1986).

[11] Studies by Armstrong (1989) and Singh et al. (1990) using both real data and randomly-generated data find that categorical matching is as good or better than alternative statistical matching procedures which are based on distance functions or random selection. Luttman (1990) provides a description of these alternative procedures.

[12] McGuckin and Nguyen (1990) demonstrate that some techniques of "masking" data to protect privacy have the advantage of not altering parameter estimates from ordinary least squares regressions. Unfortunately, they do not discuss micro-record aggregation.

[13] Up to seven such variables were used: province, age group, sex, marital status as taxed (married claiming spousal credit, married not claiming spousal tax credit, etc.), total income class (excluding capital gains), employment income class, and number of children eligible for the child care expense deduction. Often, a much lesser number of variables was used in order to provide a sufficient number of records in the bin to allow good estimates of the distributional statistics discussed in the next footnote.

bin.[14] Then, a series of random draws were made from this distribution in order to impute a value for each variable for every record on the SCF.

The result of these statistical matching techniques is that none of the tax data is raw data directly transcribed from the tax returns of particular individuals. This precludes the use of the SPSD/M for some types of studies, such as Nigrini's (1992) work on measuring the prevalence of tax evasion in particular line items by examining the distribution of the digits.

Statistical Analysis Using the SPSD/M

One advantage which the SPSD/M has over the U.S. Individual Tax Model Files for statistical analyses is that the SPSD/M probably has more variation in personal marginal tax rates for given levels of income. This reduces the multicollinearity problem noted by Crum (1991). The reason for this variation is that the provincial tax rates are not only sizeable but also vary across provinces, and the SPSD/M includes a full provincial tax calculation. Currently the provincial rates range from 44% to 62% of federal tax, and provincial surtaxes and tax credits add further variation.

Researchers undertaking statistical analysis with the SPSD/M should note that like the U.S. Individual Tax Model Files, the SPSD/M is a stratified sample and not a simple random sample.[15] For example, high-income people are over-represented in order to improve the estimate of total tax payable in the population. As Christian (1991) emphasizes, ordinary least squares (OLS) estimates of regression parameters are biased if the dependent variable is related to the variables on which the sample has been stratified. However, this problem can be corrected using a weighted least squares procedure.

The manner in which the SPSD/M has been created restricts its potential uses. As Statistics Canada states, "Statistical analysis on [this] database must be carried out with a great deal of caution, since the records do not represent observations in the ordinary sense of the word" (Wolfson et al. 1987). There are two dimensions to this problem (Wolfson et al. 1987, Statistics Canada 1987).

First, consider statistical analyses which use only variables relating to one of the four component databases. This type of analysis should generally be quite reliable since categorical matching preserves not only the univariate distributions of the variables but also the inter-variable correlations (since all variables on the same donor record are transferred together). However, the special techniques used to

---

[14] For any particular tax variable, the following figures were used to define its statistical distribution (density function): the proportion of taxpayers having non-zero values for that variable; the values for deciles 1 through 9; the mean of the bottom and top decile groups; and, in order to represent the maximum and minimum values for the variable while protecting confidentiality, the mean of the highest 5 values and the mean of the lowest 5 values. A uniform density function was assumed for the middle eight decile groups, while a Pareto (lognormal) density function was used for the highest and lowest decile groups in order to preserve appropriately-shaped tails.

[15] This property is inherited from the four component databases. An important part of the statistical matching process is the construction of an appropriate set of sample weights for each unit in the sample.

merge the Green Book database cause one or the other of these two desirable properties to be lost. For the income-tax-specific (item 7) data, the inter-variable correlations have been changed but the univariate distributions should be correct, while for the income-receipts (item 4) data the problem is reversed.

The problem with the income-tax-specific data is that although stochastic imputation takes care to replicate the univariate distributions, each variable is separately imputed and therefore the inter-variable correlations are not preserved. On the other hand, the problem with the income-receipts data is that micro-record aggregation causes the univariate distributions of the synthetic records to tend to have less variance than the original Green Book records. For example, for sparse items such as capital gains, the records to be aggregated contain several zeros which are included in the average. The average is maintained but the distribution is biased towards the mean.

Second, consider statistical analyses involving more than one of the four component databases, which the creation of the SPSD/M was intended to facilitate. In this case, the problems of single-database analyses noted above carry over, and a new problem is added—the conditional independence assumption. The difficulty is that statistical matching forces the distributions of the variables in the different databases to be independent for any given values of the variables used for matching the databases. Suppose, for example, one is interested in estimating a regression equation which predicts the amount of charitable donations from the taxpayer's education and other factors. Charitable donations is from the Green Book file, while education is from the SCF. The construction of the SPSD/M assumes that for given values of the variables used to merge the two databases (age, sex, province, income, etc.) there is no correlation between charitable donations and education. This conditional independence assumption seems unlikely to be true.[16]

Studies by Singh et al. (1990) and others show that the conditional independence assumption which underlies statistical matching procedures has the potential to seriously distort the relationship between variables from different component databases. This poses three questions. First, is the resulting difference in regression parameter estimates large enough to be of importance? Ruggles and Wolff (1977) find limited evidence that it is not. Second, is there any alternative inference methodology which can correct for this problem? Goel and Ramalingam (1989, iii) note that this possibility is "still to be resolved." Third, is it possible that future versions of the SPSD/M could relax the conditional independence assumption while still satisfying privacy concerns? Studies by Armstrong (1989) and Singh et al. (1990) show that this may be possible if auxiliary information can be used to guide the statistical matching. The auxiliary information could be a specially-conducted small-scale survey or an exact match of confidential datafiles, such as Alter (1988) does for the SCF and Green Book databases.

---

[16] For further discussion of this assumption, see Luttman (1990).

Simulation Using the SPSD/M

Like the Individual Tax Model Files, the SPSD/M can also be used for disaggregated simulation analyses of the effects of given tax changes on horizontal equity, vertical equity and aggregate tax revenue. This is a natural use for the SPSD/M because microdata files are ideal for examining the complex interactions among different aspects of the tax law caused by a package of tax changes. Generally the SPSD/M does not include any behavioural response to tax changes, but this could be added by a user if appropriate assumptions could be found.[17]

Simulation analyses are quite easy to execute on the SPSD/M because it contains a set of tax-and-transfer calculation algorithms which include several hundred parameters that can be reset to model the most common types of tax changes. Few users have so far had such sophisticated and extensive policy changes to simulate that they have needed to make changes to the source code of the algorithms, although this would be fairly easy because the source code is fully documented and written in the C language. One-way frequency tables and cross-tabulations can be produced within the SPSD/M, but the data would have to be transferred to an external package such as SAS to do regression analysis or any analysis which requires much sorting (e.g., Gini coefficients). The SPSD/M's facility for writing output files in native SAS format is quite useful in this regard. Another useful facility loads the tables produced by the SPSD/M into Lotus 1-2-3 for further analysis.

Since simulation analyses typically study the effect of tax changes in the present and future, the current version of the SPSD/M has a built-in capacity to be projected to represent any year from 1984 to 1992. Part of this projection involves moving from the year in which the data was collected to the current year, while another part involves moving from the current year to the year which is to be modelled. The issues involved are similar in both cases, although the information available is likely to be poorer in the latter case.

One of the projection issues is changing the tax and benefit calculation algorithms as required. Changes in tax law parameters are generally not difficult to model, but it is often impossible to model tax law changes which affect the computation of the tax base (e.g., changes in the types of expenses which qualify for the child care expense deduction) without making heroic assumptions. In part this is because the SPSD/M has a much smaller number of variables relating to income tax than either the Green Book file on which it is based or the U.S. Individual Tax Model Files. The age of the data is also part of the problem. For example, since the current version (4.1) of the SPSD/M uses income-tax-specific variables from the year 1984 but the lifetime capital gains deduction was not introduced until 1985, there is no information about amounts of the deduction that has been used in past years. Hence the cumulative limit on the deduction cannot be implemented in the model, so current-year deductions will be overstated.

---

[17] A useful model to follow in modelling labour-supply response is Blundell et al. (1987), who use tax and benefit-program rules to construct the full non-convex budget set faced by each household. A labour supply equation is then used to optimize labour supply within this set.

Projection issues arising from demographic and economic changes have been dealt with using the method of static aging. In particular, demographic changes are represented in the SPSD/M by varying the sample weights of each record in the database to model the year in question. Although in principle this should include many demographic variables, only the distribution by age, sex and province has been corrected because that is all that is available between census dates. Economic growth and inflation are represented by specifying growth rates of all of the various dollar-denominated income and expenditure items. The default growth rates can be changed by the user, and in version 5.0 the sample weights will also be under user control.

One problem with the current projection method in the SPSD/M is that it does not take into account the fact that the year on which the data is based and the year of the projection may represent different stages of the business cycle. For example, the current version of the SPSD/M uses 1986 data, and 1986 was a growth year in Canada with a relatively low incidence of unemployment. For a projection to the recession year of 1991, it would be desirable to increase the sample weights of the unemployed. Such business-cycle effects could be important for studies concerning the effect of taxes on the distribution of income.[18] Work on this problem is underway at Statistics Canada, and an alternative set of weight files is to be released with version 5.0.

Potential Applications of the SPSD/M

Subject to the above limitations, the SPSD/M can be used for any of the purposes for which similar U.S. tax microdata files have been used. For example, one could study the distributional impact of the 1987 Canadian personal and corporate income tax changes by applying to Canada the methodology used by Wallace, Wasylenko and Weiner (1991) to impute corporate income taxes to individuals. More generally, one could use the SPSD/M to do studies which are not possible with U.S. data because of the lack of demographic and social science variables (Luttman 1990).

Other potential areas of research may be suggested by the following list of applications of the SPSD/M to date in the tax area. All of these are simulation exercises.

- Maslove (1989) shows the distributive impacts of the changes in the personal income tax system from 1984 to 1988, while Grady (1990a) and Grady (1991a) update and expand this work.
- Brooks (1990) analyzes the effect of increasing the federal surtax instead of imposing a Goods and Services Tax, and Grady (1990b) analyzes the combined effect of the tax reform package actually legislated (the introduction of the Goods and Services Tax and the increases in the surtax and the sales tax credit). Gillespie (1991) criticizes Grady's methodology and Grady (1991b) replies.
- Mills (1990) developed a proposal for a flat tax system.

---

[18] The same criticism also applies to projections with the U.S. Individual Tax Model Files.

- Morrison and Oderkirk (1991) examine the horizontal equity of the tax system with regard to married couples vs. common-law couples.
- Wolfson and Murphy (1990) examine the taxation of the family under various taxation and transfer programs and reveal the equivalence scales that are implicit in current taxes and transfers.
- Murphy (1990) finds that families in rural areas pay relatively lower taxes and receive higher transfers than their urban counterparts.
- Murphy and Wolfson (1991) examine the expected burdens on the public sector of the major taxes, cash transfers and in-kind benefit programs in Canada over the next 40 years.

Since the SPSD/M has only been available for three years, many more studies can be expected. Future studies will be listed in Statistics Canada's publication *SPSD/M News* as they appear.

Another avenue of research is to investigate the quality of the simulation results produced by the SPSD/M and other microsimulation models. This seems quite appropriate since the conditional independence assumption and other statistical issues should affect the quality of simulations. Citro and Hanushek (1991) argue that far too little research has been undertaken into the quality of the results produced by such models:

> Can the policy analyst be reasonably confident that the estimated cost of a proposed policy change of, say, $25 billion lies within a relatively narrow bound, such as, say, $22 billion to $28 billion? Or, given the limitations of available knowledge, must the analyst acknowledge that the likely range is much wider—say from $1 billion to $49 billion—and hence that the estimate is of much less utility as a guide to decision making?

Citro and Hanushek suggest three types of validation studies:

- external validity studies in which, for example, revenue projections made prior to the enactment of a tax change are compared and reconciled to the amount of revenue actually collected (e.g., Sunley and Weiss 1991);
- sensitivity analyses that assess the effects of alternative assumptions on the estimates; and
- "computer-intensive sample reuse techniques such as the bootstrap that measure the variance of model estimates."

A further type of validation study for the SPSD/M would be to compare the results it generates to those produced by the Green Book file itself (although obtaining access to the Green Book file would be a problem). Also, one could model the same set of tax changes for the same year with two different versions of the SPSD/M (e.g., one based on 1986 data and one based on 1988 data). Using this method, Statistics Canada has found that the estimates of revenue costs change much more than the conclusions about distributional effects, which suggests that the estimates of revenue costs are one of the less reliable model outputs.

Other Data Sources

Statistics Canada also has in-house databases of personal tax returns on which it may be willing to do statistical runs for researchers on a cost-recovery basis. In particular, a researcher who is concerned with the statistical properties of the

SPSD/M or who needs extra tax variables might seek to have an analysis performed on the original Green Book file. Also, a researcher interested in panel data could possibly use the longitudinal 1982-86 family-income database which Statistics Canada prepared for a study in progress by the Economic Council of Canada on the nature and causes of poverty in Canada. This database was constructed by linking individual tax returns to create family income and then merging the resulting data with social assistance records.[19]

Statistics Canada also has corporate tax data. Annual cross-sections of detailed corporate tax returns and associated financial statements are available for the years 1969-84. More recent data is available only in a less accessible form. Statistics Canada is currently using inter-corporate ownership data to link corporations in an enterprise structure, i.e., linking parents and subsidiaries. This data could be used, for example, for a study of the determinants of corporate charitable donations. Although this data is not likely to be publicly released, Statistics Canada might perform computer runs on this data on a cost recovery basis. Statistics Canada also might be willing to consider a research partnership in which access to data is provided free provided that the researcher supplies the manpower to do the work on-site in Ottawa and results of interest to Statistics Canada can be expected. For further information, contact the Analytical Studies Branch of Statistics Canada at the address noted in footnote 6 above.

Aggregate data from the Green Book file of personal tax returns is published in Revenue Canada's annual publication *Taxation Statistics*. The latest edition, which was issued in late 1991, covers 1989 tax returns. The level of detail of income sources and deductions is roughly equivalent to that in the SPSD/M. Two recent studies which used this data source are Howard, Ruggeri and Van Wart (1991) and Van Wart and Ruggeri (1990).[20] Aggregate data from Statistics Canada's database of corporate tax returns appears in their annual publications *Corporation Taxation Statistics* and *Corporation Financial Statistics* (Statistics Canada catalogue numbers 61-208 and 61-207 respectively). This data has been used by Douglas (1990).

An alternative to Statistics Canada as a source of Canadian personal and corporate income tax data is the federal Department of Finance, which is the main body in Canada responsible for tax policy. The Department's own employees are sometimes allowed to publish studies using its microdata files (Glenday et al. 1986 and Kitchen and Dalton 1990), but access by outside authors is permitted quite infrequently. The only such published works are Venti and Wise (1988) and Clarkson Gordon Foundation (1991). The Department has been much less reluctant about releasing aggregate statistics, such as those required to calculate marginal effective tax rates by industry (Daly et al. 1987). It is possible that a provincial government might be less reluctant to allow access to its microdata.[21]

---

[19] For more information, contact the Small Area and Administrative Data Division, Informatics and Methodology Branch, Statistics Canada.

[20] For further information, phone (613) 957-7387 or write to: Personal Taxation Statistics and Modelling, Statistical Services Division, Revenue Canada Taxation, Head Office, Ottawa K1A 0L8.

[21] Many provinces have personal income tax microdata, but (surprisingly) only Ontario has such data for corporate income tax, and it has just acquired it this year.

Canada has no counterpart to the U.S. Taxpayer Compliance Measurement Program data. According to Revenue Canada (undated), which is a document released under the Canadian Access to Information Act in 1990,

> [Revenue Canada] developed a Compliance Measurement System in the late 1970's and captured three years of data. The results were similar to the American experience. However, the process was not continued, and the results have never been considered to be reliable for planning purposes.

Canada also has no counterpart to the U.S. Tax Practitioner Survey and Taxpayer Opinion Survey.

A final source of data is financial statements of companies. Compustat and Compact Disclosure have versions for Canadian companies. Thornton (1987) used financial statement data to study effective tax rates on inflation-adjusted income.

REFERENCES

Alter, H. 1988. Linked Records as a Foundation for Analysis. Staff report, Labour and Household Surveys Analysis Division, Statistics Canada: Ottawa.

Armstrong, J. 1989. An Evaluation of Statistical Matching Methods. Methodology Branch Working Paper BSMD 90-003E, Statistics Canada: Ottawa.

Atkinson, A. B., and H. Sutherland, eds. 1988. *Tax-Benefit Models*. STICERD, London School of Economics and Political Science.

Beam, R. E., and S. N. Laiken. 1991. *Introduction to Federal Income Taxation in Canada, 12th Edition 1991-92*. Toronto: CCH Canadian.

Blundell, R., C. Meghir, E. Symons, and I. Walker. 1987. A Labour Supply Model for the Simulation of Tax and Benefit Reforms. R. Blundell and I. Walker, eds. *Unemployment, Search and Labour Supply*. Cambridge, England: Cambridge University Press.

Bordt, M., G. Cameron, S. Gribble, B. Murphy, G. Rowe, and M. Wolfson. 1990. The Social Policy Simulation Database and Model: An Integrated Tool for Tax/Transfer Policy Analysis. *Canadian Tax Journal* (January/February): 48-65.

Brooks, N. 1990. Searching for an Alternative to the GST. Discussion Paper No. 90-C-1, Institute for Research on Public Policy: Ottawa.

Christian, C. W. 1991. Endogenous Sampling in the Statistics of Income Panel of Individual Returns. *Journal of Economic and Social Measurement*.

Citro, C., and E. Hanushek, eds. 1991. *Improving Information for Social Policy Decisions: The Uses of Microsimulation Modelling*. Washington: National Academy Press.

Clarkson Gordon Foundation. 1991. *Policy Options for the Treatment of Tax Losses in Canada*. Toronto: Thomson.

Cotton, P., and G. Sadowsky. 1989. Future Computing Environments for Socioeconomic Microsimulation. Paper prepared for the National Academy of Sciences Panel to Evaluate Microsimulation Models for Welfare Programs.

Crum, R. P. 1991. Statistics of Income Panel of Individual Returns: An Overview. C. Enis, ed., *A Guide to Tax Research Methodologies*. American Accounting Association.

Daly, M., J. Jung, P. Mercier and T. Schweitzer. 1987. The Taxation of Income from Capital in Canada: An International Comparison. *Canadian Tax Journal* (January/February): 88-119.

Douglas, A. 1990. Changes in Corporate Tax Revenue. *Canadian Tax Journal* (January/February): 66-81.

Enis, C. 1991. The Use of Individual Tax Model Files to Obtain Data for Empirical Research in Taxation. C. Enis, ed., *A Guide to Tax Research Methodologies*. American Accounting Association.

Flesher, T. undated. Statistics of Income bibliography. Unpublished paper, University of Mississippi.

Gillespie, W. I. 1991. How to Create a Tax Burden where No Tax Burden Exists: A Critical Examination of Grady's 'An Analysis of the Distributional Burden of the Goods and Services Tax'. *Canadian Tax Journal* (Issue no. 4): 925-936.

Glenday, G., A. Gupta, and H. Pawlak. 1986. Tax Incentives for Personal Charitable Contributions. *Review of Economics and Statistics* (November): 688-693.

Goel, P., and T. Ramalingam. 1989. *The Matching Methodology: Some Statistical Properties.* Springer-Verlag.

Grady, P. 1990a. The Distributional Impact of the Federal Tax and Transfer Changes Introduced Since 1984. *Canadian Tax Journal* (March-April): 286-297.

————. 1990b. An Analysis of the Distributional Impact of the Goods and Services Tax. *Canadian Tax Journal* (May/June): 632-643.

————. 1991a. Taking Stock of Tory Tax Reform. Paper presented at the 1991 annual meeting of the Canadian Economics Association, Kingston, Ontario.

————. 1991b. The Distributional Impact of the Goods and Services Tax: A Reply to Gillespie. *Canadian Tax Journal* (Issue no. 4): 937-946.

Howard, R., G. Ruggeri, and D. Van Wart. 1991. The Progressivity of Provincial Personal Income Taxes in Canada. *Canadian Tax Journal* (Issue Number 2): 288-308.

Kalton, G., and D. Kasprzyk. 1986. The Treatment of Missing Survey Data. *Survey Methodology*: 1-16.

Kitchen, H., and R. Dalton. 1990. Determinants of Charitable Donations by Families in Canada: A Regional Analysis. *Applied Economics*: 285-299.

Lietmeyer, V. 1986. Microanalytic Tax Simulation Models in Europe: Development and Experience in the German Federal Ministry of Finance. G. H. Orcutt, J. Merz, and H. Quinke, eds., *Microanalytic Simulation Models to Support Social and Financial Policy.* Elsevier: Amsterdam.

Luttman, S. 1990. Enriching Tax Research through Database Merging. *The Journal of the American Taxation Association* (Spring): 68-75.

Maslove, A. M. 1989. *Tax Reform in Canada: The Process and Impact.* Institute for Research on Public Policy: Ottawa.

McGuckin, R. H., and S. V. Nguyen. 1990. Public Use Microdata: Disclosure and Usefulness. *Journal of Economic and Social Measurement*: 19-39.

Mills, D. 1990. *The Single Tax.* Hemlock: Toronto.

Morrison, R. J., and J. Oderkirk. 1991. Married and Unmarried Couples: The Tax Question. *Canadian Social Trends* (Summer): 15-20.

Murphy, B. 1990. The Distribution of Federal/Provincial Taxes and Transfers in Rural Canada. Rural and Small Town Canada: Economic and Social Reality: A Conference.

————, and M. C. Wolfson. 1991. When the Baby Boom Grows Old: Impacts on Canada's Public Sector. *The Statistical Journal of the United Nations Economic Commission for Europe* 8 (No. 1): 25-44.

Nigrini, M. 1992. The Detection of Income Tax Evasion through an Analysis of Digital Distributions. Ph.D. thesis proposal, University of Cincinnati.

Organization for Economic Co-operation and Development. 1988. *A Comparative Study of Personal Income Tax Models.* Committee on Fiscal Affairs, OECD.

Revenue Canada Taxation. undated. Final Report of the Committee on the Restructuring of Compliance Programs. Unpublished.

Ruggles, N., and E. Wolff. 1977. Merging Microdata: Rationale, Practice and Testing. *Annals of Economic and Social Measurement*: 407-28.

Singh, A. C., H. Mantel, M. Kinack, and G. Rowe. 1990. On Methods of Statistical Matching With and Without Auxiliary Information. Methodology Branch working paper SSMD-90-016E, Statistics Canada: Ottawa.

Smeeding, T., L. Rainwater, J. Coder, G. Schmaus, and C. de Tombeur. 1988. Luxembourg Income Study: Information Guide. LIS-CEPS working paper #7 (write to: LIS at CEPS/ INSEAD, Case Postale 65, L-7201 Walferdange, Gr. D. Luxembourg).

Statistics Canada. 1987. SPSD Database Creation Technical Reference Manual. Unpublished. Statistics Canada: Ottawa.

Sunley, Emil D., and R. Weiss. 1991. The Revenue Estimating Process. *Tax Notes* (June 10): 1299-1314.

Sutherland, H. 1991. Constructing a Tax-Benefit Model: What Advice Can One Give?*Review of Income and Wealth* (June): 199-219.

Thornton, D. B. 1987. Inflation, Accounting and the Canadian Corporate Tax Base. *Canadian Journal of Administrative Sciences* (March): 66-96.

Van Wart, D., and G. C. Ruggeri. 1990. The Effects of Tax Reform on the Elasticity of the Personal Income Tax. *Canadian Tax Journal* (October): 1210-1226.

Venti, S., and D. Wise. 1988. The Determinants of IRA Contributions and the Effects of Limit Changes. Z. Brodie, J. Shoven, and D. Wise, eds. *Pensions in the U.S. Economy.* University of Chicago Press and National Bureau of Economic Research.

Wallace, S., M. Wasylenko, and D. Weiner. 1991. The Distributional Implications of the 1986 Tax Reform. *National Tax Journal* (June): 181-198.

Wolfson, M., S. Gribble, M. Bordt, B. Murphy, and G. Rowe. 1987. The Social Policy Simulation Database and Model: An Example of Survey and Administrative Data Integration. *Statistical Uses of Administrative Data: An International Symposium.* Statistics Canada, Ottawa: 201-9.

——, ——, ——, ——, and ——. 1989. The Social Policy Simulation Database and Model: An Example of Survey and Administrative Data Integration. *Survey of Current Business* (May): 36-40.

——, and B. B. Murphy. 1990. The Role of Equivalence Scales in Canadian Public Policy. Paper presented to "Familles et niveaux de vie: observations et analyse," a conference of the European Association for Population Studies, Barcelona.

Chapter 5
Congressional Information Service Statistical Indexes

Adrianne E. Slaymaker
Wayne State University

The Congressional Information Service was established in 1970 to provide access to the publications of Congress, including the Congressional Budget Office and the Office of Technology Assessment (except those reported in the *Congressional Record*). The objective of this chapter is to provide an overview of the four major indices of published statistical information available from the Congressional Information Service (CIS).

In 1970, CIS began its first publication, the *Congressional Information Service Index* (*CIS/Index*). This index covers all publications of the U.S. Congress, including those of the Senate and House Appropriations Committees, some of which are not cited by the Government Printing Office's *GPO Monthly Catalog*.[1] In 1971 the President's Commission on Federal Statistics recommended that a second publication be provided to index all the statistical publications of the U.S. Government excluding the Congressional publications abstracted in the *CIS/Index*. In response to this need, the *American Statistics Index* (*ASI*) was established in 1972 to index information from all federal government agencies. A third publication, the *Statistical Reference Index* (*SRI*) was established by CIS in 1980 to index information available from state and local government agencies in the U.S., some foreign government agencies, plus private statistical references provided by industry organizations and others. With different focuses, the *ASI* and *SRI* are highly complementary with very little overlap in coverage. The last of the CIS's four publications, the *Index to International Statistics* (*IIS*), was begun in 1983. The *IIS*'s objective is to index English language statistical publications of the world's major international intergovernmental organizations (IGOs). It contains the smallest number of abstracts of the four publications, covering UN, OECD, EC, OAS and about 80 other organizations.

The structure and use of the four indices is similar; they differ primarily in their information targets. As the largest of the four, the *CIS/Index*'s focus on Congressional publications, statistical information and legislative history, differentiates it from the other three indices. The *ASI*, *SRI* and *IIS* are almost identical, differing only in the sources of the statistical information cited.[2] The *CIS/Index* and *ASI* annual

---

[1] The *GPO Monthly Catalog*, published by the U.S. Government Printing Office provides bibliographic information for publications by U.S. government authors identified by name and address of the issuing agency, and arranged by Superintendent of Documents (SuDoc) classification number.

[2] Two CD-ROM products were introduced by CIS in 1989 to allow users to search the four indices. The *Congressional Masterfile 2* is a set of two disks with all abstracts, indexes and legislative histories from the *CIS/Index* since 1970. Due to their similarity, the *ASI*, *SRI*, and *IIS* can be searched simultaneously by use of the Statistical Masterfile. (For more information contact the CIS Marketing Department in Bethesda, MD.)

volumes include federal government publications during the year while the *SRI* and *IIS* annual volumes include publications reviewed during the year. Thus for 1989 publications the researcher would choose the 1989 volumes for the *CIS/Index* and *ASI*, and the 1990 volumes for the *SRI* and *IIS*. The next section of this chapter describes the organization and statistical resources covered in the *ASI*, *SRI*, and *IIS*. The following section briefly explores the coverage of the somewhat different *CIS/Index*. The final section of this chapter illustrates coverage and use of the four indices, including data retrieval information.

The *ASI*, *SRI*, and *IIS*

The *ASI*, *SRI*, and *IIS* services are provided in two volumes: (1) Abstracts and (2) Index. The Abstract volume provides the user with a brief overview and citation to the statistical resource. The Index volume contains four or five indices to the annotations in the Abstract volume. The following provides a guide to the information available and use of the *ASI*, *SRI*, and *IIS*.[3] (A list of the major topics of interest to the tax researcher found in the *ASI* and *SRI* is included in Exhibit 1.)

The years covered by the *ASI* in the various two volume sets include (*ASI* xvii):
* Retrospective Edition (1960-1973)
* Annual Editions—each with single year coverage (1974-1990)
* Monthly Supplement Editions for the current year.
* Multi-Year Cumulative Indexes
    - 1974 to 1979 (published May 1990)
    - 1980 to 1984 (published 1985)
    - 1985 to 1988 (published 1989)

SRI's first multiple-year cumulation covers 1980-85, the second 1986-89, with annual volumes for the following years and monthly supplements for the current year. *IIS*'s coverage begins in 1983; there is one multiple year cumulation (1983-87), with annual index volumes for the following years. A 1988-91 *IIS* cumulation will be published in December 1992.

Coverage of the *ASI*, *SRI* and *IIS*

ASI covers the six major federal publishing agencies plus additional departments and agencies, special program related and other statistics as follows (*ASI* xviii):

* **Agricultural Statistics Board, Department of Agriculture** - Monthly to annual reports on every important U.S. crop, with data on production, yield, prices, prospective plantings, and indicated production for the season.
* **Bureau of the Census** - Decennial census of population and housing; quinquennial economic and agricultural censuses; Census of Governments; Current Housing Reports, Current Industrial Reports, monthly foreign trade data, and reports from the monthly Current Population Survey; and methodological studies, indexes, and guides.

---

[3] The following information has been extracted or quoted with permission of the publisher, from the Users Guide which introduces all four Indexes *(Copyright CIS, all rights reserved)*. Found at the front of both volumes of each Index for all years, the Users Guide provides a more detailed description of the coverage, organization, and use of the Index, plus information for data retrieval.

EXHIBIT 1
Major Subjects in the *ASI* and *SRI* of Interest to Tax Researchers

- Accounting and Auditing
- Balance of Payments
- Bureau of the Census
- Bureau of Economic Analysis
- Business Assets/Liability
- Business Formation
- Business Income and Expenses
- Checking Accounts
- Consumer Credit
- Corporations
- Credit
- Debt
- Department of Commerce
- Department of Treasury
- Depreciation
- Distribution of Income
- Domestic International Sales Corporations
- Earnings
- Economic Development
- Employment and Unemployment
- Estate Tax
- Excise Tax
- Family Income
- Federal Asset and Disposition Assoc.
- Finance/Finance Companies
- Financial Institutions
- General Accounting Office
- Gift Tax/Gifts and Private Contribution
- Government Forms and Paperwork
- Gross National Product
- Income Taxes
- Individual Retirement Arrangements
- Interest Payments
- Investments
- Joint Taxation
- Liquor/Liquor Industry
- Lobbying/Lobbying Groups
- National Income and Product Accounts
- Partnerships
- Pensions and Pension Funds
- Personal and Household Income
- Projections and Forecasts
- Property Tax/Value
- Proprietorships
- Real Estate Business
- Research and Development
- Sales Tax
- Severance Taxes
- Social Security Tax
- State and Local Taxes
- Tariffs and Foreign Trade Controls
- Tax Courts of the U.S.
- Tax Credits
- Tax Delinquency/Evasion
- Tax Exempt Securities
- Tax Expenditures
- Tax Incentives/Shelters
- Tax Laws/Courts
- Tax Loopholes
- Tax Protests/Appeals
- Tax Reform
- Tax Sharing
- Taxation
- U.S. International Trade Commission

---

* **Bureau of Labor Statistics** - Monthly reports on the Consumer Price Index and unemployment rate; and other periodic, serial, and annual reports on prices, wages and hours, benefits, collective bargaining, work stoppages, and productivity.

* **Energy Information Administration** - Weekly to annual reports on U.S. production, consumption, stocks, trade, and prices of all major energy resources; finances and operations of oil companies, electric utilities, and other energy industries; and projections of energy supply and demand.

* **National Center for Education Statistics** - Annual and other collections of data on elementary, secondary, and higher education schools, staff, students, finances, curricula, and graduates.

* **National Center for Health Statistics** - Monthly and annual collections of vital statistics; and periodic surveys of the health condition of the population, and of health care, personnel, and facilities.

* **Other Departments and Agencies** - Primary data from required reports and special surveys from other agencies such as the Bureau of Mines, Justice Department, Treasury

Department income tax statistics, Federal Reserve data on finances and banking, Department of transportation and National Science Foundation.

* **Program Related Statistics** - Executive department and administrative or regulatory agency statistics on funding and programs covering agency financial statements, personnel, processing efficiency, workloads, payments made etc. including areas such as social security recipients and payments, food stamp recipients, aliens admitted, speed of handling court cases, etc. and the *Budget of the U.S.*
* **Special Studies** - Monographs, analyses, and studies which include statistical data of probable research value including a number of reports by the General Accounting Office.
* **Non-Tabular Statistics Related Materials** - Narrative, charts, listings, maps etc. that provide aid in locating statistical data or in understanding statistical programs.

ASI does not include scientific and technical engineering, clinical medical, and animal laboratory data found through other services; private organization contract studies, Congressional publications (except those that contain substantial statistical information);[4] and classified and confidential U.S. data.

The sources of data for the *SRI* consist of over 1,000 organizations including trade, professional, and other nonprofit associations and institutes, business organizations, commercial publishers, independent research organizations, state government agencies and universities and affiliated research centers. Selection of these sources is based on (*SRI* xix):

* **Review of Secondary Sources** - "Directory of Business and Financial Services," "Business Information Sources," "Guide to Special Issues," and "Indexes of Periodicals" and numerous other bibliographies.
* **Harvard University Baker Library** industry statistics file.
* Canvass of National Associations with annual budgets over $1 million.
* Canvass of business-oriented periodicals in order of sales in Folio 400.
* Canvass of 2,000 State Government agencies to identify offices publishing the most comprehensive reports on state administered programs.
* Consultations with librarians who are specialists in information fields such as banks/ finance, state documents and others.
* Follow-up references cited in current periodicals and other news media.

In selecting items for coverage *SRI* includes (*SRI* xx):

* Publications presenting business, industrial, financial, and social statistics of general research value, and having national, regional, or statewide breadth of coverage. Where there is redundancy of content among groups or related series of publications, emphasis is placed upon selecting those publications presenting time series or regularly updated statistics, and those with the most comprehensive, detailed coverage.
* Publications containing statistics in subject areas or in geographic detail not well covered by Federal data, and statistics useful for comparison with Federal data.
* Publications presenting data that, while in some respects limited in scope, geographically or otherwise, are the best or most authoritative found for a given subject, or present a unique analysis or statistical base.

SRI does not include highly localized data, scientific or highly technical data, publications for which microfiche reproduction rights cannot be obtained, publications restating Federal data without analysis, and publications of municipal and

---

[4] Congressional abstracts can be found in the *CIS/Index to Publications of the U.S. Congress.*

county governments.[5] Additionally, securities data and quotations intended primarily for investment purposes are excluded.

The *IIS* focuses primarily on the world's major publicly available IGO English language statistical publications, covering over 1,850 titles. The statistics covered include (*IIS* v-vi):

* **Primary data** on business and finance, economic development, agriculture, foreign trade, transportation and communication, energy, health, employment, education, government, and natural resources.
* **Research data** of general interest, or on a limited subject judged to have research value beyond the limited area of coverage.
* **Secondary data** presented for analytic or comparative purposes.
* **Bibliographic and methodological works** that substantially aid in the understanding and use of statistical publications, including those presenting historical benchmark or base statistics for time series covered on a current basis by *IIS*.
* **Program and budget statistics** of IGOs, where these are annual reviews or assessments, or provide substantial current information on an agency's activity in individual countries or specific areas of endeavor.

Excluded from coverage are IGO internal administrative data, highly scientific or technical research data, and localized data of limited interest.

The Indices for Annotation Retrieval

There are five basic indices in the *ASI* used to locate the abstracts for the statistical publications. The five indices and their content are (*ASI* xx):

Subject and Name Index which answers questions like "What publications provide statistical data on research and development?" and "What publications were issued by the Office of Management and Budget?" These references are based on:
- Subjects of Publications
- Place Names of Cities, Counties, States, Foreign Countries
- Government Agency Names
- Major Government Programs and Proposals
- Special Classes of Publications or data
- Individual Personal Names, Companies and Institutions
- Major Surveys

Category Index which answers questions such as "What publications provide cost of living data broken down by city, or some other geographic category?" and contains references to citations based on:
- Geographic Categories
- Economic Categories
- Demographic Categories

The *Title Index* contains references to federal government publications by title. Included are:
- Publications in Annual Editions
- Periodical Articles
- Conference Papers
- Larger Publications with Separate Abstracts

---

[5] Certain municipal and county government publications can be found in the *Index to Current Urban Documents* published by Greenwood Press, Westport, CT.

The *Agency Report Number Index* cites annotations based on Report Number given by the Issuing Agency. This index would be used, for example to locate reports in the Bureau of Labor Studies Bulletin 30XX series.

The *SuDoc Number Index* cross-references the *ASI* abstracts to SuDoc numbers.[6]

A Guide to Selected Standard Classifications used within the *ASI* by government agencies is contained in the back of the Index volume. This guide provides information such as:
*   Census Regions and Divisions
*   Metropolitan Statistical Areas (MSAs)
*   Consolidated Metropolitan Statistical Areas
*   Consumer Price Index Cities
*   Standard Industrial Classification (SIC) Code (2 digits)
*   Standard Occupational Classification Code (1 to 3 digits)
*   Standard International Trade Classification (SITC) Code (3 digit)

In the *SRI*, three of the four Indices, the Subject Index, Category Index and Title Index are very similar to the *ASI*, including the same subheadings in the Category Index. The Issuing Source Index is similar to the Agency Index of the *ASI* and contains the name of issuing sources in natural word order, including all associations, business organizations, commercial publishers, independent research organizations, state agencies and university departments or research centers whose publications have been abstracted and indexed by *SRI*. The last part of the Index volume contains the same Guide to Selected Standard Classifications found in the *ASI*.

The *IIS* has a Subject Index, Category Index and Title Index similar to those of the *ASI* and *SRI*. Additionally, like the *SRI*, the *IIS* has an Issuing Source Index. Similar to the *ASI*'s SuDoc number index, the *IIS* has a Publication Number Index for EC, OAS, and UN publications.

When using the Index volumes of all CIS publications, the researcher should be aware that the following conventions exist (*ASI* xxiv-xxv):
*   Alphabetization follows Library of Congress practice.
*   Alphabetization is on a word-by-word basis.
    Ex. "New Jersey" and "New York" precede "Newark," and "Fire Departments" precedes "Firearms."
*   Proper names are entered in natural word order.
    Ex. you will find "Department of Labor" rather than "Labor Department." Names of individuals always have last name first.
*   References to the United States - U.S. is an implied prefix. You will find "Army" rather than "U.S." Army. In Agency titles, "U.S." has been dropped except where necessary to conform to U.S. Government Manual usage.

Congressional Information Service Index

The *Congressional Information Service Index* contains three volumes: (1) Abstracts, (2) Index and (3) Legislative History. The objective of the *CIS/Index* is to cite

---

[6] Superintendent of Documents (SuDoc) numbers, like Library of Congress (LC) numbers for nongovernmental publications, organize U.S. government publications within the Government Depository Libraries. Neither system is exclusive and some publications have both LC and SuDoc numbers.

the more than 800,000 pages published per year by the nearly 300 Congressional committees, subcommittees and special offices. These publications contain transcripts of testimony from public and Government witnesses, plus exhibit reports, statistical data, articles, specially commissioned studies, analyses of federal legislation and activities, and compilations of background materials.

CIS/Index's coverage begins with 1970. However, earlier years can be found in the following additional CIS Congressional and Legal Services volumes. The *CIS U.S. Serial Set Index* indexes a complete collection of congressional reports and documents issued from 1789 through 1969. The *CIS Index to U.S. Senate Executive Documents and Reports* covers confidential Senate Executive Documents and reports dealing with treaties and nominations. The *CIS U.S. Congressional Committee Prints Index* contains over 15,000 Congressional committee prints[7] from the early 1800s through 1969. The *CIS U.S. Congressional Committee Hearings Index* abstracts over 40,000 hearings from the early 1800s through 1969. The *CIS Index to Unpublished U.S. Senate Committee Hearings*, *CIS Index to Unpublished U.S. House of Representatives Committee Hearings*, and *CIS Index to Presidential Executive Orders and Proclamations, 1789-1983* index even more information not contained in the *CIS/Index*.[8]

The Congressional Publications Covered

As noted previously, the *CIS/Index* contains abstracts of six major types of Congressional publications not found in the *Congressional Record* as follows (*CIS/Index* viii-x).

* **Hearings** - Public hearings held by committees to gather opinions and information regarding the desirability of legislation, to fulfill annual oversight responsibilities, or to investigate specific reports or charges of executive branch activities.
* **Committee Prints** - Research staff and outside consultant publications which provide situation reports, statistical or historical information and legislative analyses.
* **House and Senate Reports** - Committee Reports with recommendations concerning the findings of hearings and deliberations for the House and/or Senate.
* **Documents** - Presidential messages, the texts of various executive agencies' annual or special reports to Congress.
* **Executive Reports and Treaty Documents** - The text of Presidential communication supporting ratification and the text of the treaty.
* **Public Laws** - All Public Laws as they are finally enacted including the text, codified references to portions of statutes amended, and a brief list of related House and Senate Reports and floor actions.
* **Special Publications** - Occasional materials such as a compilation of all Federal laws on social security.

The Index Volume

Like the *ASI*, *SRI*, and *IIS*, the *CIS/Index* contains a Subject and Name Index and a Title Index. The Subject and Name Index differs somewhat from those of the *ASI*,

---

7 Committee prints are studies and reports printed to aid Congressional committees in their legislative and oversight activities (*CIS/Index* viii).
8 These volumes are part of the 36-volume CIS U.S. Serial Set Index and CIS U.S. Serial Set on microfiche collection, available in some libraries containing the *CIS/Index*.

SRI, and *IIS*, covering the names and affiliations of witnesses, the names of outside authors (individuals and corporations), and names of the subcommittee holding hearings or issuing publications. There is no Category Index because Congressional publications are not broken down into geographic, economic and demographic categories. The Title Index lists the titles of all congressional publications alphabetically in natural word order for proper names, omitting initial articles, and editing where necessary. Additionally, *CIS/Index* has an Index of Bill, Report, Document, Hearings, and Print Numbers and an Index of Committee and Subcommittee Chairman not found in the other three publications.

The Legislative Histories Volume

The third volume in the *CIS/Index* series contains abstracts and legislative histories for all nonceremonial public laws enacted during the year of coverage. This volume includes basic bibliographic information for the law, the text of the law, and an annotation of the law's chief provisions, and significant "riders." For "major legislation" the legislative intent based on detailed research is provided, including citations to all relevant bills and debates to assist with research used for litigation.

Use of the *ASI, SRI, IIS* and *CIS/Index*

The last section of this chapter illustrates the use of the *ASI, SRI, IIS*, and *CIS/Index*. For our example, let's assume that the tax researcher has identified research and development (R&D) for this search. While the researcher will be interested in a specific aspect of this broad topic, the following discussion concentrates on providing insight into the method and type of data to be found in the CIS publications. Thus, citations from the Index volumes in this illustration have been chosen for their diversity of publisher, at the expense of concentrating on a singular aspect of R&D.

Our search for information on R&D is divided into four steps: I) choice of year; II) choice of index and obtaining the abstract citation; III) location of the abstract; and IV) retrieval of the data. Once again the discussion will begin with the *ASI* and continue with the *SRI, IIS* and *CIS/Index*.

After choosing a specific year,[9] the researcher generally chooses the Subject Index from the Index volume to obtain an abstract of the publication. If the tax researcher was interested in developing a project comparing R&D by state, the Category Index would be used to develop a list of sources. The *CIS/Index* has an abstract browsing advantage which differs from the other three indices. Whereas the *ASI, SRI*, and *IIS* abstracts are organized by issuing source, the *CIS/Index* Abstracts volume is organized by Congressional committee. The researcher may choose to browse through committee publications, such as those for the House Ways and Means Committee to locate documents. A second attraction of the *CIS/Index* allows

---

[9] For this example the most recent full year set available in the summer of 1991 was chosen for each index. Thus the 1989 volumes were used for the *ASI* and *CIS/Index*, and the 1990 volumes were used for the *SRI* and *IIS*.

the researcher to directly access legislative histories in the third volume when the Public Law number is known.

For this example the Subject Index in the *ASI* provides a list of 39 sources, and seven cross references to other subjects for the topic **Research and Development**. The *SRI*'s coverage of private, and state and local sources of statistics, provides an additional list of 114 sources, and six cross references to other subjects. The *IIS*'s Subject Index produces another 52 sources of data and five cross references for **R&D**. Unlike the searches in the other three Indexes, the *CIS/Index* search under **Research and Development** references only other key words. From the three choices, **Research** is chosen and a list of 122 sources is obtained.

The lists generated from all four of the Subject Indexes include a short description of each of the 327 sources. The description includes an accession number to locate each abstract in the Abstract volume of the different CIS publications. For this example let's say that the tax researcher reads through the four lists from the Index volumes and chooses the descriptions in Exhibit 2 for further review.

The next step is to locate the abstract for each publication chosen for further review. The abstracts are arranged in the Abstract volume by accession number. Each of the CIS publications has a unique system assigning accession numbers. These numbers provide a uniform citation to the abstracts in the Abstract volume

---

EXHIBIT 2
Index Descriptions for the Research and Development Search

From the *ASI*
> Expenditures for R&D by source and field, selected years 1953-89, annual rpt, 9624-18.

From the *SRI*
> Industrial R&D activities and quality assurance, articles and special features, monthly rpt, C1850-6.
>
> Corporate R&D expenditures, and sales and profits for approx 900 US and 200 leading foreign firms, 1989, annual feature, C5800-7.232.
>
> Japan R&D expenditures by performing sector, and natural science research expenditures by purpose, FY84-89, article, R5650-2.220

From the *IIS*
> EC R&D activities, with cost estimates and budget allocations, by research type, as of Dec 1989, EC rpt feature, 1300-P29.7.
>
> US econ analysis, with R&D spending by selected sector; and nontariff trade controls by selected commodity; with comparisons to other OECD countries, 1970s-86, OECD annual rpt, 2300-S2.126.

From the *CIS/Index*[*]
> Business R&D expenditures tax credit extension, H263-3, H782-38, S361-21, PL101-239 (Title VII).

---

[*] From the Subject Index under **Research**. Use of the Legislative History volume would have found similar information under **Tax Incentives and Shelters**.

through all years of publication. Thus, once an accession number has been obtained for one year, the publication can be found in other years' Abstract volumes without consulting the Index volume. The discussion in the next part provides an overview of the accession number conventions for each CIS publication, followed by its application to the description chosen from the Index volume list.

The *ASI*'s accession number is based on the following (*ASI* xx):

* **Issuing Agency** (1st 2 to 4 digits of Accession Number)
* **Publication Type** (Last digit before hyphen)
    - 2 = Current Periodicals, Daily Through Semi-Annual
    - 4 = Annuals and Biennial
    - 6 = Publications In Series
    - 8 = Special and Irregular Publications
    - 1,3,5,7,9 = Special Series and Special Groups of Publications
* **Sequential ASI Serial Number** (digits after hyphen)
* **Analytic Number** (decimal no's following main abstract accession number)

The R&D publication selected from the *ASI* list is:

Expenditures for R&D by source and field, selected years 1953-89, annual rpt, 9624-18.

Applying the above conventions to the **9624-18** accession number found at the end of the description, the first three numbers **962** refer to the National Science Foundation (NSF); **4** refers to an annual/biennial publication; the sequential *ASI* Serial Number is **-18**. No analytic number is given by the index. However, the Abstract Volume contains tables from the publication numbered 1-5.

The *SRI*'s accession numbers are based on the following (*SRI* xxiv-xxv):

* **Type of Issuing Source** - The initial Letter of Accession Number
    - A = Associations
    - B = Business organizations
    - C = Commercial publishers
    - R = Independent research centers
    - S = State agency or subagency
    - U = Universities and affiliated research organizations.
* **Individual Issuing Source** - four digits following the initial letter, up to the hyphen.
* **Sequential SRI serial number** - The digits after the hyphen.
* **Analytic number** - references analytic abstracts, identified by a decimal number at the end of the accession number.

The three examples chosen from the *SRI* are:

Industrial R&D activities and quality assurance, articles and special features, monthly rpt, C1850-6.

Corporate R&D expenditures, and sales and profits for approx 900 US and 200 leading foreign firms, 1989, annual feature, C5800-7.232.

Japan R&D expenditures by performing sector, and natural science research expenditures by purpose, FY84-89, article, R5650-2.220

The accession numbers **C1850-6**, **C5800-7.232**, and **R5650-2.220** locate these three in the Abstract volume. The initial reference letter **C** refers to a commercial publication and **R** to an Independent Research Center. The number **1850** refers to

Cahners Publishing Co. and **-6** refers to its *R&D* publication; **5800-7** refers to McGraw Hill's *Business Week*; and **5650-2** to the Japan Economic Institute's *JEI Report*. The numbers following the decimal indicate the issue of the publication, with **.232** referring to the June 15, 1990 issue of *Business Week*, **.220** to the "1990 Update on Japanese Research and Development" in the September 28, 1990 issue. The lack of numbers in the first annotation indicates that all of the published issues of *R&D* are appropriate.

The *IIS*'s accession numbering system has the following characteristics (*IIS* vi-vii):

* The first four numbers pertain to the IGO issuing publication in alphabetical sequence based on the full, spelled-out name.
* The letter following identifies publication types as follows:
  - D = Documents
  - M = Monographs or special one-time publications
  - P = Periodicals
  - S = Serials
* The three digits after the letter pertain to the IIS sequential serial number which provides a unique identification for each publication.
* The final subordinate decimal number describes individual reports within a series (if any).

The two descriptions chosen from the *IIS* list are:

EC R&D activities, with cost estimates and budget allocations, by research type, as of Dec 1989, EC rpt feature, 1300-P29.7.

US econ analysis, with R&D spending by selected sector; and nontariff trade controls by selected commodity; with comparisons to other OECD countries, 1970s-86, OECD annual rpt, 2300-S2.126.

The accession numbers at the end of the *IIS* examples catalog the European Community as **1300**; its periodical bulletin **-P29** has specific data sources located in the Research and Technology Issue **.7**. **2300** refers to the Organization for Economic Cooperation and Development (OECD)'s annual economic survey **-S2**; **.126** describes the OECD Economic Survey of the United States for 1988/89.

The *CIS/Index* accession numbers refer to the Abstracts volume and/or the Legislative Histories volume. Since the *CIS/Index*'s focus is on Congressional publications, the accession numbers in the Abstract volume begin with an **H, J,** or **S** to designate the House, Joint Committee or Senate parent body issuing the document. The two numbers following the Congressional committee letter refer to specific publications of the parent body. The third number indicates the publication type as follows (*CIS/Index* x-xi):

> 0 = House or Senate Document or Special Publication
> 1 = Hearing
> 2 = Committee Print
> 3 = House or Senate Report
> 4 = Senate Executive Report
> 5 = Senate Treaty Document

Every Abstract volume accession number is then followed by a dash and a serial number. The Legislative Histories volume accession numbers begin with a Public

Law designation, **PL**, followed by the Congressional session number, public law number and title.

The example chosen from the *CIS/Index* is:

> **Business R&D expenditures tax credit extension, H263-3, H782-38, S361-21, PL101-239 (Title VII).**

This example contains four accession numbers. The first three accession numbers reference abstracts in the Abstract volume, beginning with **H** for House and **S** for Senate. The fourth reference's **PL** is found in the Legislative Histories volume. Using the above convention, **H263-3** refers to House (**H**) Budget Committee (**26**) Report (**3**) number 3 (**-3**), the *Omnibus Budget Reconciliation Act of 1989*; **H782-38** annotates House Ways and Means Committee (**78**) Committee Print (**2**) number 38, a description by Chairman Rostenkowski relating to provisions of the bill, including the R&D credit; and **S361-21** annotates Senate Finance Committee Hearing number 21, July 12, 1988 on miscellaneous tax bills. **PL101-239 (Title VII)** references the Legislative History volume for Title VII of Public Law number 239 of the 101st Congress, entitled the *Revenue Reconciliation Act of 1989* passed December 19, 1989 (seventeen pages of annotated legislative history).

The Abstracts and Publication Retrieval

The abstracts retrieved provide the researcher with a description of the data contained in the publication and retrieval information. The last part of this section provides 1) a summary of the information found in the CIS publication's abstract, 2) the actual R&D abstract for this example, and 3) describes how to use the information given in the abstract to obtain the data.

The abstracts found in the *ASI* contain information about the specific data in the publication: source, level of detail, relation of the publication to other statistical series, time span and geographic coverage, periodicity of data collection and publication, outline of physical contents, titles of tables, review continuity and length of time series data with references to earlier publications in the series, and information concerning related publications. References to the publication include: SuDoc number (where possible), Library of Congress (LC) card number (where applicable), the Government Printing Office (GPO) Monthly Catalog number and/or the GPO Stock number (if listed), and/or the Depository Item Number.

The publication cited in the R&D example from the *ASI* (shown in Exhibit 3) contains a narrative summary with charts and tables plus appendices with detailed tables. A hardcopy of the source can be found in a U.S. Government Depository Library using the SuDoc number **NS1.22/2:989**. Using the Library of Congress number **LC 80-645057** the publication can be found either in the researcher's library collection or through interlibrary loan. If a GPO stock number (S/N) had been provided the publication could be purchased, while the supply lasts, from the Government Printing Office, at the price given in the abstract.[10] If the tax researcher's

---

[10] The GPO stock number and price of publications which can be purchased are also located in the *GPO Monthly Catalog*.

EXHIBIT 3
Abstract from the 1989 *ASI* — Research and Development

9624-18 NATIONAL PATTERNS OF
R&D RESOURCES, 1989 Annual.
Jan. 1989. v+72 p. NSF 89-308. •Item
834-T. ASI/MF/3 °NS1.22/2:989. LC
80-645057

By John E. Jankowski, Jr. Seventh
annual report on science and technology R&D and basic research expenditures and employment in Federal, academic, and industrial sectors, 1950s-89. Data are compiled
from NSF and other Federal agency
publications. Contents: narrative summary, with 18 charts and 3 tables (p.
1-29); and appendices, with 36 detailed tables, listed below (p. 33-72).
No separate report was issued for
1988. Previous report, for 1987, was
titled *National Patterns of Science
and Technology Resources* (see 1988
Annual under this number).

---

library does not have the publication, *ASI* provides a microfiche Library collection by *ASI* accession number, available at most libraries which subscribe to *ASI*. Here, **ASI/MF/3** indicates that the R&D publication is available on the third *ASI* microfiche for 1989.

Like the *ASI*, the *SRI* abstracts contain information about the specific data that is presented: source, level of detail, contents summary, description of the statistical information, and availability of the information. Plus, *SRI* abstracts provide an overview of the publication including: principal subject/purpose, major data topics, geographic areas, and time periods covered by data. This is illustrated in the *SRI* abstracts from the R&D example shown in Exhibit 4.

Here, the source of the data abstracted is noted including information on availability, price, International Standard Serial Number, Library of Congress number and *SRI* microfiche availability. The *R&D* example pertains to a monthly publication covering R&D funding, management and new product developments and applications. This statistical source can be located by its ISSN[11] **0746-9179** or Library of Congress number **LC 84-642292**. While the supply lasts the source may be purchased from the publisher R&D, 44 Cook St., Denver, CO, for $10. A final alternative is to use the accession number for the 1990 *SRI* Microfiche Library

---

[11] ISSN refers to the International Standard Serial Number assigned or authenticated by the National Serials Data Program. Each number is unique to a title and is part of the international effort for uniform control of serials.

EXHIBIT 4
Abstracts from the 1990 *SRI* — Research and Development

C1850-6 R&D
Monthly. ISSN 0746-9179. LC 84-642292. SRI/MF/excerpts, shipped quarterly.

Monthly publication reporting trends and developments in industrial design and quality assurance. Covers R&D funding, management, and new product developments and applications. Issues contain regular editorial depts; news articles on scientific and technological developments; and feature articles, occasionally statistical. Annual features include an R&D funding forecast, and surveys of R&D professionals' salaries. Please note that title has changed from *Research and Development*, beginning with the Jan. 1990 issues. Features with substantial statistical content are described, as they appear, under "Statistical Features." Each issue of the journal is reviewed, but an abstract is published in SRI monthly issues only when statistical articles appear. *Availability*: R&D, 44 Cook St., Denver, CO 80206-5800, qualified subscribers, others $49.95 per yr., back issues $10.00 each; SRI/MF/excerpts for all portions described under "Statistical Features;" shipped quarterly. Issues reviewed during 1990; Nov. 1989-Oct. 1990 (P) (Vol. 31, Nos. 11-12; Vol. 32, Nos. 1-10).

C5800-7 BUSINESS WEEK
Weekly ISSN 0007-7135. LC 31-6225. SRI/MF/not filmed

C5800-7.232: June 15, 1990 (No. 3164) [Special issue price is $3.95. Issue number is omitted.]

R&D SCOREBOARD; GLIMPSING THE FUTURE IN THE NUMBERS, ANNUAL FEATURE

(p. 194-223) Annual feature on R&D expenditures and financial performance of 894 U.S. companies grouped by industry (20 broad industry groups, with detail for numerous subgroups), 1989. Also includes data for 11 R&D consortia, and top 200 foreign companies in R&D spending. Data were compiled by Standard & Poor's Compustat Services, Inc.
  Contents:
a. Narrative analysis, with 3 summary tables; 6 tables showing 5 industries with highest and lowest percent increase in R&D spending, top 10 companies ranked by 3 measures of R&D spending, and foreign R&D spending summary by country, 1989; and tabular list of 11 U.S. R&D consortia, including purpose and 1990 funding. (p. 194-196)
b. Tabular list of U.S. companies grouped by industry, showing the following for each: R&D spending and sales (total and per employee), and profits, 1989, with percent change from 1988, and ranking within industry and comparisons to 1985-89 period for R&D spending per employee. (p. 197-217)
c. Index of U.S. companies. (p. 217-219) *d.* Tabular list of top 200 foreign companies ranked by R&D spending, with sales and profits (all in U.S. dollars), 1989. (p. 220-222)

e. Index of foreign companies. (p. 223) **R5650-2 JEI REPORT**
Weekly, in 2 parts. Approx. 10 p. ISSN 0744-6489. LC sn82-20877. SRI/MF/excerpts, shipped quarterly.

R5650-2.220: Feb. 2, 1990 (No. 5B) JAPAN'S TRADE SURPLUS FALLS FOR THIRD YEAR QUARTERLY FEATURE

(p. 4-7) Quarterly article, with 4 tables showing value of Japan's exports and imports in dollars and yen, for total and U.S. bilateral trade, annually 1985-89 and quarterly 1987-89.

Japanese Research Spending Rises
(p. 8-10) Article, with 2 tables showing Japan's R&D expenditures, by performing sector (companies, research institutions, and universities); and natural science research expenditures, by purpose (basic, applied, and developmental); FY 84-88. Data are from Japan's Management and Coordination Agency.
  For description of related articles, see SRI 1989 Annual under R5650-2.126 and R5650-2.142.

collection, which should be available at most libraries which subscribe to *SRI*, to obtain excerpts from R&D. A general description including the ISSN and LC numbers, and *SRI* microfilm information are provided in the annotations of the other two sources of data.[12]

Each resource abstract from the *IIS* contains an ISSN number. Unlike the publications cited in the *ASI* and *SRI*, *IIS* publications may not be readily available in the U.S. Thus, these publications may not contain an LC number for retrieval (see Exhibit 5 for the two examples cited above).

From this example, the *Research and Technology* data is located in Volume 22 No. 12 of the *Bulletin of the European Communities*. It can be found in print using the ISSN number **0378-3693** or the LC number **79-19603**. Unless the researcher's library has an extensive collection, neither reference may be available. Fortunately, the *IIS* microfiche collection contains 95 percent of the resources annotated. For the libraries which do not subscribe to the international publications abstracted, retrieval of this publication through the 1990 *IIS* microfiche collection is the most practicable. As a final alternative, the publication can be ordered from Unipub in Luxembourg.

The abstracts found in the *CIS/Index* differ stylistically from those of the *SRI*, *ASI* and *IIS*, but maintain the overall objective of summarizing the subject matter (not the conclusions). *CIS/Index* abstracts cite the date of issue/hearing/passage; the Congress and Session; and identifying document numbers which may include one or more of the following: two SuDoc numbers, one for print and one for microfiche; Library of Congress number; GPO Monthly Catalog number and/or GPO document number and price; House or Senate hearing/report number; and CIS Microfiche number. The annotations in the Legislative History volume usually refer only to the document's print SuDoc number (if any) and/or CIS Microfiche number. See Exhibit 6 for the example abstracts.[13]

Information retrieval is once again dependent on the available library facilities. While the major documents have numerous alternative citations, documents that do not appear in the GPO Monthly Catalog (and do not receive SuDOC numbers), like Chairman Rostenkowski's description **H782-38**, are available only from the *CIS/Index* Microfiche.

Summary

The Congressional Information Service publishes four major indices of public and private data. The four publications are complementary and cover the majority of federal, state and local governmental sources of data and information, private

---

[12] *Business Week* is widely circulated, thus was not filmed for the SRI microfiche collection. On the other-hand, both *R&D* and *JEI Report* are shipped quarterly on microfiche.

[13] The legislative history of the R&D credit is not included in Exhibit 6 due to its 17 page length. The R&D credit is a rather small portion of the overall tax act's citation contained in the Legislative History's references to: the House Report; Senate Bill (S.2484) from the 100th Congress; hearings on July 12, 1988 (including testimony from many named persons), hearings on April 12, 1989 (witness names provided); Joint Taxation Committee Prints issued March 13, 1989 and April 7, 1989, plus the Conference Comparison prepared by the Joint Taxation Committee; and other documents.

EXHIBIT 5
Abstracts from the 1990 *IIS* — Research and Development

1300-P29 BULLETIN OF THE EUROPEAN COMMUNITIES
Monthly. Approx. 135 p. [En]
CB-AA-(yr)-(nos.)-EN-C.
ISSN 0007-5116 (printed as ISSN 0378-3693). LC 79-19603. IIS/MF

Monthly report (with July/Aug. and occasional other combined issues) on activities of EC institutions. Includes data on financing operations, draft and final budget appropriations and resources, development assistance projects, food assistance, and emergency aid; and information on economic, foreign, and administrative policy actions, and Court of Justice cases and decisions.

Also includes review of EC steel industry performance, often with data on supply/demand, quota/output comparisons, quarterly rates of abatement for establishment of quotas, or production expectations for related industries, with some data by country.

Also includes data on ECU exchange rates against selected currencies, and conversion rates into EC national currencies in connection with EC common agricultural policy.

Special features with substantial statistical content, including annual analyses, are described and indexed in IIS as they appear; those reviewed for this IIS issue are described below.

Data sources: Primarily EC Commission sources.

Format and data presentation: Contents listing; 2-7 brief articles; report, with text statistics and 2 exchange rate tables; and subject index.

Selected data are shown by country.

Data time coverage: Reports are issued approximately 3-6 months after month shown on cover. Data and information on EC activities are primarily for cover month. Budget data are shown for current year, with occasional plans or comparisons to previous year; budget drafts are shown as of cover month. Steel industry data variously cover most recent available quarter or other period, or selected forecasts or trends.

Note: A series of supplementary reports is also issued (covered in IIS under 1300-S67).

Availability: Unipub (Lanham), EC (Luxembourg), $110.00 per yr.; IIS/MF.

Issues reviewed during 1990: 1989 (Vol. 22, Nos. 2-12); 1990 (Vol. 23, No. 1/2).

1300-P29.7: 1989 (Vol. 22, No. 12) RESEARCH AND TECHNOLOGY

(p. 35-38) Reviews EC R&D activities. Includes data on cost estimates for R&D framework program, by research type; and budget allocations for human genome analysis, and research on nuclear waste management; as of Dec. 1989.

Includes 3 tables.

2300-S2 OECD ECONOMIC SURVEYS
Annual Series. For individual bibliographic data, see below. [En] ISSN 0376-6438. IIS/MF

2300-S2.126: OECD Economic Surveys, 1988/89. United States [Annual Series. 1989. 148 p. Foldout. (Sales No. 10 89 02 1) ISBN 92-64-13304-6. LC 77-642793. IIS/MF.]

Includes data on industrial capacity utilization; troubled and insolvent savings and loan institutions; tax reform impact on government revenues; foreign investment; investment in automation; R&D spending; nontariff trade controls; sales and employment concentrations of largest 100-500 firms; and share in number and sales of largest corporations worldwide; varying periods 1959-89 with selected forecasts to 1992.

Also includes data on business mergers and acquisitions; high yield corporate debt issuance related to leveraged buyouts; foreign ownership of business assets; assets and liabilities of financial institutions and nonfinancial sectors; services trade; and exports of selected technology intensive commodities.

Most indicator tables show data for varying years 1975-88 with selected quarterly data for 2nd quarter 1988-2nd quarter 1989.

Data sources: OECD country review as of Oct. 18, 1989.

EXHIBIT 6
Abstract from the 1989 *CIS/Index* — Research and Development

H263-3 OMNIBUS BUDGET RECONCILIATION ACT OF 1989. Sept. 20, 1989. 101-1. iii+1555 p. il. GPO $33.00 S/N 052-071-00881-1.CIS/MF/18 •Item 1008-C; 1008-D. H. Rpt. 101-247. °Y1.1/8:101-247.

Recommends passage of H.R. 3299, the Omnibus Budget Reconciliation Act of 1989, to amend the Agricultural Act of 1949 and numerous other acts. Incorporates recommendations of 10 House Committees for reducing outlays and increasing revenues for FY90 spending programs, as required by the concurrent FY90 budget resolution.

Committee recommendations are incorporated in the following titles:

Title I, Agriculture Committee, including farm program revisions. Exempts from sequestration under the Balanced Budget and Emergency Deficit Control Act of 1985 payments made by the Department of Treasury to the Farm Credit System Financial Assistance Corp.

Title II, Banking, Finance, and Urban Affairs Committee, including reauthorization of FEMA flood and crime insurance programs.

Title III, Education and Labor Committee, including provisions regarding the Stafford Student Loan Program, restrictions on employer termination of defined benefit pension plans, expansion of Headstart Project and establishment of a new early childhood development and school-based care program, and grants to States for child care service for infants, toddlers, and young children and child care coordinating activities. Title III, Subtitle A, Chapter 1 is cited as the Student Loan Reconciliation Amendments of 1989; Subtitle B is the Miscellaneous ERISA Amendments Act of 1989; Subtitle E is the Early Childhood Education and Development Act of 1989; Subtitle E, Chapter 3 is the Child Care Services for Infants, Toddlers, and Young Children Act; and Subtitle E, Chapter 4 is the Child Care and Early Childhood Development Coordinating Activities Act.

Title IV, Energy and Commerce Committee, including provisions regarding medicare, health care research and policy, medicaid, maternal and child health, NRC user fees, SEC fees, and FCC fees and fairness doctrine requirements. Subtitle C, Part B is cited as the Child Health Amendments; Subtitle C, Part C is the Community and Facility Habilitation Services Amendments; and Subtitle C, Part D is the Frail Elderly Community Care Amendments.

Title V, Government Operations Committee, including provisions regarding Postal Service Fund off-budget status.

Title VI, Interior and Insular Affairs Committee, including provisions regarding NRC user fees, increased oil shale claims receipts, and revisions in funding and management of Forest Service timber programs in the Tongass National Forest in Alaska.

Title VII, Merchant Marine and Fisheries Committee, including provisions regarding DOT imposition of fees on cruise and gambling vessels, ocean protection fees on outer continental shelf leases, Panama Canal Commission (PCC) escrow fund interest, PCC authorization for FY90, and authorization for PCC civilian employees to use military commissaries.

Title VIII, Post Office and Civil Service Committee, including provisions regarding Postal Service Fund off-budget status and modification of USPS payments for retirement cost-of-living adjustments and health benefits.

Title IX, Veterans' Affairs Committee, including provisions regarding Department of Veterans Affairs home loan guarantee program.

Title X, Ways and Means Committee, including provisions regarding social security and Railroad Retirement System, establishment of SSA as an independent agency, medicare, foster home care and child welfare programs, child support enforcement, poor elderly assistance programs, trade and tariff provisions, and Caribbean Basin economic recovery initiatives. Subtitle E is cited as the Caribbean Basin Economic Recovery Expansion Act.

Title XI, Ways and Means Committee, including provisions regarding capital gains tax treatment, extension of the telephone excise tax, employee stock ownership plans, the Airport and Airway Trust Fund, imposition of an excise tax on ozone-depleting chemicals, tax treatment of corporate mergers and acquisitions which increase corporate debt, Internal Revenue Code civil penalties, modification of the earned income tax credit to account for family size, and extension of various tax incentives, including the low-income housing credit, the business research tax credit, employer-provided education assistance, the targeted jobs tax credit providing employer incentives for hiring handicapped and economically disadvantaged workers, and the energy credit for business geothermal property. Subtitle G is cited as the Improved Penalty Administration and Compliance Tax Act. Also

(Continued on next page)

EXHIBIT 6 (Continued)

includes provisions to revise non-discrimination rules applicable to certain employee benefit plans, including employer-provided health plans. Includes minority, additional, supplemental, dissenting, and additional dissenting views (p. 308-325, 619-627, 1531-1555).

H.R. 3299 is related to H.R.2771 and numerous other bills.

H782-38 DESCRIPTION OF PROPOSAL BY CHAIRMAN ROSTENKOWSKI RELATING TO CHILD CARE AND THE EARNED INCOME TAX CREDIT, Expiring Tax Provisions, Medicare Catastrophic Insurance Provisions, and Certain Other Revenue Provisions. July 18, 1989. 101-1. iii+36 p. Oversized. CIS/MF/3

Description, prepared by Joint Taxation Committee staff, of additional items to be included in the Committee Chairman's reconciliation proposal containing FY90-FY94 tax and revenue initiatives. Includes provisions to:
a. Expand the earned income tax credit for lower-income working taxpayers with dependent children to reflect family size.
b. Expand Title XX social services block grant to States for the provision of child care services.
c. Temporarily extend various expiring tax provisions, including the tax exclusion for employer-provided educational assistance and the targeted jobs tax credit.
d. Permanently extend the low-income rental housing tax credit and the research and experimentation tax credit.
e. Reduce the rate of medicare supplemental premiums enacted under the Medicare Catastrophic Coverage Act of 1988.

Reviews present law, explains proposed changes, and presents effective dates for each initiative. **S361-21 MISCELLANEOUS TAX BILLS, 1988. July 12, 1988.** 100-2. vi+396 p. GPO $12.00 S/N 552-070-05898-2. CIS/MF/ 7 •Item 1038-A; 1038-B. S. hrg. 100-1019. °Y4.F49:S.hrg.100-1019. MC 89-13791. LC 89-601919.

Hearing before the *Subcom on Taxation and Debt Management* to consider the following miscellaneous tax bills (summary, p. 62-91):
S. 1239, to exempt short-term loans extended by small banks in the normal course of business from accrual basis tax accounting requirements applicable to taxpayer short-term obligations.
S. 1821, to exclude certain skilled workers in seafood processing plants from the definition of employees for Federal withholding tax purposes.
S. 2078, to require an employee vote and majority approval prior to employer establishment of an employee stock ownership plan (ESOP).
S. 2484, the Research and Experimental Credit Extension and Reform Act of 1988, to make permanent and enhance incentives for business use of the research and experimental (R&E) tax credit.
S. 2611, to allow IRS to disclose certain tax return information to VA for the purpose of determining eligibility for and amount of means-tested veterans' pensions and other benefits.
H.R. 1961, the Pension Portability Act of 1988, to preserve pension benefits when an employee changes employment by increasing the ability of individu-

als to retain pension assets in individual retirement accounts or other tax-favored retirement vehicles.

H.R. 2792, to clarify that income earned by Indian tribal members exercising fishing rights guaranteed by treaty, statute, or Executive order is exempt from Federal and State Taxation.

Supplementary material (p. 54-396) includes submitted statements, correspondence, and witnesses' written statements.

S. 2409 listed on document cover is not discussed by witnesses.

data sources, and English language international data sources. The indices are print based with limited CD/ROM availability, and cite largely print based data sources. The information provided by the *CIS/Index* on the Congressional Committee reports, hearings, and other documents pertaining to tax legislation is not surpassed by any other source (including the GPO Monthly Catalog).

Chapter 6
Funding Opportunities for
Tax Grant Proposals

David W. LaRue and Suzanne M. Luttman
University of Virginia and Santa Clara University

The following tables provide initial information on some of the sources of funding available for tax accounting research. While not specifically stating a preference for tax research, descriptions of the work to be funded may encompass certain analyses currently being done by tax accountants. This is clearly not an exhaustive list.

The grant opportunities are divided into three categories: Table 1 for research programs available to doctoral students, Table 2 for postdoctoral work, and Table 3 for funding opportunities provided to institutions rather than to an individual (although they may include support for an individual's work).

A request for additional information about a grant/fellowship should be sent to the name and address indicated in the first column of the table. A phone number is provided where available. You may want to include information on the project for which you are seeking funding so that the granting institution can make an initial indication of the viability of the project in their program.

The second column provides the title and a brief description of the types of projects expected to be funded. The third column discusses some of the eligibility requirements for each program, and the final column provides information on the amount of the award and the application deadline. An "NA" indicates the information was unavailable.

TABLE 1
Doctoral Research Grant Opportunities

Granting Institution	Title/Topic Areas	Eligibility Requirement	Size of Award/ Application Deadline
Mr. Paul L. Gerhardt, Executive Director American Accounting Association 5717 Bessie Drive Sarasota, FL 34233-2299	*American Accounting Association Fellowship Program in Accounting.* Fellowships to assist individuals furthering their preparation, through doctoral studies, to teach in colleges and universities.	Acceptance in doctoral program (only entering candidates eligible) of school accredited by AACSB at master's level, completed application (forms, recommendation letters, GMAT scores).	$5,000 February 1
American Association of University Women Educational Foundation Programs Office 2401 Virginia Ave., N.W. Washington, DC 20037	*Dissertation Fellowships for Women of the United States.*	Women who have completed all course work and examinations for the doctorate by January 2 of fellowship year.	$12,500 November 15
American Association of University Women Educational Foundation Programs Office 2401 Virginia Ave., N.W. Washington, DC 20037	*Graduate Fellowships for Women of Countries Other Than the Unites States.*	Women pursuing graduate study or advanced research at approved institutions in the United States.	$13,000 December 1
Stephen Anspacher Academic and Career Development American Institute of Certified Public Accountants 1211 Avenue of the Americas New York, NY 10036-8775 (212) 575-8910	*AICPA Doctoral Fellowships Program* for students intending to teach accounting in the U.S.	Must apply before entering doctoral program at an accredited member school of the AACSB. Must possess a valid CPA certificate.	$5,000 April 1
Thomas J. Nessinger, Trustee Arthur Andersen & Co. Foundation 69 West Washington Street Chicago, IL 60602 (312) 580-0069	*Arthur Andersen & Co. Foundation Fellowships for Doctoral Candidates at the Dissertation Stage.* Fellowships for assistance in completing the research and writing of doctoral dissertations in accounting and related areas of tax, computer science, or other areas directly related to the firm's management information consulting practice.	Doctoral candidates at AACSB schools. Recipients must accept an obligation to teach at the university level for at least three of the first five years following termination of the award.	$12,000 March 1

(Continued on next page)

TABLE 1 (Continued)

Granting Institution	Title/Topic Areas	Eligibility Requirement	Size of Award/ Application Deadline
Deloitte & Touche Doctoral Fellowship Program Deloitte & Touche Foundation Ten Westport Road Wilton, CT 06897	**Deloitte & Touche Foundation Doctoral Fellowships** are a two-phase program consisting of (1) support in completing course work and (2) support during 12 months of the dissertation stage.	After review by the doctoral institution, no more than two ranked applications per school are forwarded to the foundation with recommendations.	$18,000 October 15
Ernst & Young Foundation Grants to Doctoral Candidates Concentrating in Accounting 787 Seventh Avenue New York, NY 10019	**Grants to Doctoral Candidates Concentrating in Accounting** to allow the recipient to devote full time to completing the dissertation.	Candidate must intend to teach accounting in the US for three years following completion, be enrolled in a doctoral program at a school accredited by the AACSB at the master's level, have a reasonable expectation of completing the dissertation within the period of payments (not to exceed one year), devote full time to the dissertation, and not receive any other financial aid except tuition, fees, and research expenses.	$18,000 maximum June 1
Neil C. Pickett Hudson Institute, Inc. Herman Kahn Center 5395 Emerson Way P.O. Box 26-919 Indianapolis, IN 46226 (317) 545-1000	**Fellowship in Domestic or International Political Economy.** Policy-oriented research assessing national and regional economic issues.	Completion of all coursework toward Ph.D., an outstanding academic record, strong recommendation, and interest in policy-oriented research and interdisciplinary analysis.	$18,000 April 30
Walter Grinder Vice President, Academic Affairs Institute for Humane Studies c/o George Mason University 4400 University Drive Fairfax, VA 22030 (703) 323-1055	**Research grants and fellowships in any area of knowledge, with emphasis on the social sciences.**	Different qualifications for the various programs.	$2,000 - 2,500 Applications accepted throughout year.

Gail Ryba Richard D. Irwin Foundation 1818 Ridge Road Homewood, IL 60430	*Richard D. Irwin Foundation Doctoral Fellowships* for prospective teachers in business, economics, and the social sciences.	Candidates for a doctorate at schools with an accredited doctoral program who have completed all work except writing the dissertation and passing final oral exams. Must be nominated by Dean (direct applications from candidates not accepted).	$1,500 - 2,500 February 15
Elizabeth Ernst, Foundation Administrator KPMG Peat Marwick Foundation Doctoral Scholarship Program Three Chestnut Ridge Road Montvale, NJ 07645	*KPMG Peat Marwick Foundation Doctoral Scholarship Program* is available to assist candidates for doctoral degrees at universities in the US. The *Walter Sutton Scholarship* is granted to candidates at midwestern universities.	Scholarships are paid to students in the second year of their doctoral program. Student must possess at least two years of meaningful business experience, submit application and supporting documents, and be endorsed by the administrator of the doctoral program.	$10,000 March 15
Kenneth W. Hunter, Coordinator Doctoral Research Program Training Institute United States General Accounting Office 441 G Street, N.W. Room 7822 Washington, DC 20548 (202) 275-8673	*U.S. General Accounting Office Doctoral Research Program* for students willing to become actively involved in GAO work while gathering data for their dissertations.	Must have completed all prerequisites for candidacy, be a U.S. citizen, be willing to move to Washington, DC for the period of employment, and be willing to sever ties violating conflict of interest laws.	$24,705 - 29,891 February 1

TABLE 2
Postdoctoral Research Grant Opportunities

Granting Institution	Title/Topic Areas	Eligibility Requirements	Size of Award/ Application Deadline
American Association of University Women Educational Foundation Programs Office 2401 Virginia Ave., N.W. Washington, DC 20037	*Postdoctoral Research Fellowships for Women.* Also available: one *Founders Fellowship* awarded to woman of outstanding scholarly achievement.	Postdoctoral research to women holding doctorate at time of application. Preference to people holding degree for at least three years.	$15,000 November 15
Antony T. Sullivan, Program Officer Earhart Foundation 2200 Green Road, Suite H Ann Arbor, MI 48105	*Earhart Foundation Fellowship Research Grants* supporting such disciplines as government/political science and economics.	Professionally established individuals associated with educational and/or research institutions. Effort should lead to advancement of knowledge through teaching, lecturing, and publication.	$300-22,500 (average=$7,552) 120 days prior to commencement of projected work period.
Ernst & Young Foundation Tax Research Grant Program Beverly R. Tierney Administrative Coordinator 1950 Roland Clarke Place Reston, VA 22091-1490	*E&Y Tax Research Grant Program* supports promotion of objective tax research in accountancy. Areas of interest include policy, planning, history, education, compliance, and comparative systems.	Must be accounting faculty member holding full-time teaching appointment and possess terminal degree qualifications as prescribed by AACSB.	Maximum $50,000 November 15
Peter R. Weitz, Director of Programs German Marshall Fund of the United States 11 Dupont Circle, N.W. Suite 750 Washington, DC 20036 (202) 745-3950	*German Marshall Research Fellowship Program* for research projects on the comparative political, economic, and social aspects of both domestic and international issues.	Fellowship program for research concerned with contemporary problems of industrial societies. Project must have U.S. and European components.	NA November 15
Peter R. Weitz, Director of Programs German Marshall Fund of the United States 11 Dupont Circle, N.W. Suite 750 Washington, DC 20036 (202) 745-3950	*German Marshall Short-term Grants for Transatlantic Travel* to encourage interaction between the world of scholarly analysis and the world of practical action.	For participation as a discussant or presenter of paper at conference.	NA No less than six weeks before the conference date.

Contact	Description / Eligibility	Amount / Deadline
Wendy S. Minkin Program Administrator National Fellows Program Hoover Institution Stanford University Stanford, CA 94305-6010 (415) 723-0163	**Hoover Institution on War, Revolution and Peace**. Fellowship for one full year of unrestricted, creative research and writing at the Hoover Institution. Preference for proposals embodying empirical studies of significant public policy issues confronting the United States. Must hold Ph.D., have 3-4 years experience beyond doctorate, and have clear indications of intellectual competence. Fellows are expected to complete a full-length manuscript during residency.	Average stipend is $26,000. Second Monday in January.
Walter Grinder Vice President, Academic Affairs Institute for Humane Studies c/o George Mason University 4400 University Drive Fairfax, VA 22030 (703) 323-1055	**Institute for Humane Studies** research grants and fellowships in any area, with emphasis on the social sciences. Various programs have different eligibility requirements.	$2,000 - 2,500 Applications accepted throughout year.
Dr. Dimitri Papadimitriou, Executive Director Jerome Levy Economics Institute Brad College Annandale-on-Hudson, NY 12504 (914) 758-7448	**Jerome Levy Economics Institute Resident Fellowships**. Funding is for economic research which will lead to better economic policy. Fellows will spend the year working at the institute devoting full time to their research. Fellows provided with extensive support including computer hardware and software, access to resources, secretarial services, etc.	Salaries are competitive. Accepts applications for one-year resident fellowships to begin in each June or September.
Elizabeth Ernst, Foundation Administrator KPMG Peat Marwick Foundation Three Chestnut Ridge Road Montvale, NJ 07645-0435 (201) 307-7151	**KPMG Peat Marwick Foundation Tax Research Opportunities Program**. Restricts grants to educational purposes related to its firm's functional areas.	Range from $500 - 50,000 October 15
Elizabeth Ernst, Foundation Administrator KPMG Peat Marwick Foundation Three Chestnut Ridge Rd. Montvale, NJ 07645 (201) 307-7151	**KPMG Peat Marwick Foundation Research Fellowships** assist accounting faculty members who have demonstrated interest, ability, and productivity in attaining tenure and ultimately national recognition. Individual must possess a doctorate and have held an untenured, full-time tenure-track position at a university in the U.S. for no less than 18 months and no more than 48 months.	$25,000/year for two years. March 15

(Continued on next page)

TABLE 2 (Continued)

Granting Institution	Title/Topic Areas	Eligibility Requirements	Size of Award/ Application Deadline
Ann Brownell Sloane, Manager National Center for Automated Information Retrieval 165 East 72nd Street Suite 1B New York, NY 10021 (212) 249-0760	*National Center for Automated Information Retrieval.* Grants for research in information technology that may affect the delivery of law and accounting services. Also awards an occasional senior research fellowship.	NA	$8,000 - 40,000 NA
Mr. Peter De Janosi Russell Sage Foundation 112 East 64th Street New York, NY 10021 (212) 750-6000	*Russell Sage Foundation Postdoctoral Fellowships* support promising research on political and social problems of the U.S. by enabling young scholars to undertake a year of intense research and writing.	Must be nominated by senior faculty member who may be a colleague of the nominee or a scholar at another institution. Nominees should be assistant professors who have already made a contribution to an area of research and shown superior promise.	Academic salary at time of nomination. Fellows coming from outside NY will also receive an allowance for increased living expenses. November 30 for nominations, January 15 for completed applications.
Floyd L. Williams, Chief Tax Counsel Tax Foundation 470 L'Enfant Plaza, S.W. East Building #7400 Washington, DC 20024 (202) 863-5454	*Ernst & Young - Tax Foundation Visiting Professor Program* was instituted to disseminate information from the academic community to the business community and tax policymakers.	Professors will be brought to Washington, DC to work with the Tax Foundation for three- to four-month periods. Approximately 1/2 of the time will be spent producing a major study in their field of expertise. Professors will research and write timely studies and short reports on the impact of various US tax policies.	$15,000 stipend $10,000 living allowance. January 31
Andrew Mellon Postdoctoral Fellowships Director of Graduate Programs, FAS University of Pittsburgh 910 Cathedral of Learning Pittsburgh, PA 15260 (412) 624-6094	*Andrew Mellon Postdoctoral Fellowships.* University of Pittsburgh postdoctoral fellowships for advanced study and research in various fields.	Preference given to applicants who have completed doctoral requirements by January 15. Fellows are expected to be in Pittsburgh throughout the period of their appointment.	$22,000 for 11 month appointment; $18,000 for 9 month. January 15

TABLE 3
Institutional Programs

Granting Institution	Title/Topic Areas	Eligibility Requirements	Size of Award/ Application Deadline
Hillel Fradkin Vice President for Program The Lynde and Harry Bradley Foundation, Inc. 777 East Wisconsin Avenue Suite 2285 Milwaukee, WI 53202-5395 (414) 291-9915	**The Lynde and Harry Bradley Foundation, Inc.** Supports fellowships, project grants, general operations contributions, capital campaigns, conferences and seminars, publications, research and professorships in national research and education in public policy, higher education and activities which investigate and nurture the moral, cultural, intellectual and economic institutions which form a free society.	Recipients must be registered with the IRS and hold 501(c)(3) nonprofit status.	Range from $500-$3,000,000; average is $5,000 to $150,000. Matching fund requirements are sought when appropriate. July 15, September 15, December 15, and March 15
Richard M. Larry, Treasurer The Carthage Foundation P. O. Box 268 Pittsburgh, PA 15230 (412) 392-2900	**The Carthage Foundation.** Grants primarily for public policy research.	No grants to individuals.	NA None.
Barron M. Tenny, Secretary The Ford Foundation 320 East 43rd St. New York, NY 10017 (212) 573-5000	**The Ford Foundation.** Provides grants to institutions for experimental, demonstration, and developmental efforts likely to produce significant advances in the fields of public policy and education.	No grants for routine operating costs, construction or maintenance of buildings.	Average range from $50,000 to 1,000,000. None.
Richard G. Mund, Foundation Executive Director Mobil Foundation, Inc. Room 3D809 3225 Gallows Road Fairfax, VA 22037	**Mobil Foundation Grants.** Education support is given in the area of business; programs supported include curriculum development, staff acquisition, faculty research, fellowships, and scholarships for women and minorities.	Grants are not made directly to individuals.	Range from $1,000 to $480,000. Applications are accepted at any time.

(Continued on next page)

TABLE 3 (Continued)

Granting Institution	Title/Topic Areas	Eligibility Requirements	Size of Award/ Application Deadline
Programs in Biological, Behavioral and Social Sciences National Science Foundation 1800 G St., N.W. Washington, DC 20550	*NSF - Programs in Biological, Behavioral, and Social Sciences.* The majority of support is made available for basic research, although work of a more applied nature may also be funded.	The most frequent recipients of these grants are academic institutions and nonprofit research institutions. Awards, under special circumstances, may be awarded to other types of institutions as well as individuals.	NA Proposals may be submitted at any time during the year, and applicants should allow approximately six to nine months for consideration.
Dr. Felice J. Levine, Program Director or Bonney Sheahan, Associate Program Director Law and Social Sciences Division of Social and Economic Science Directorate for Biological, Behavioral, and Social Sciences National Science Foundation 1800 G. St., N.W. Washington, DC 20550 (202) 357-7567	*NSF - Law and Social Research Grants.* Research is supported on processes that enhance or diminish compliance and the impact of law; causes and consequences of variations and changes in legal processes and institutions; personal, social, economic, technological, and cultural conditions affecting use of and responses to law; dynamics of disputing and dispute resolution mechanisms and strategies; determinants of legal decision making; effects of and factors accounting for administrative rule making and the regulatory role of law; and processes that influence the development of law and explain transformations between formal legal rules and law in action.	NA	NA January 15 and August 15
Dr. Roberta Dalstad Miller, Director Division of Social and Economic Sciences Directorate for Biological, Behavioral and Social Sciences National Science Foundation 1800 G St., N.W. Washington, DC 20550 (202) 357-7966	*National Science Foundation.* Supports basic and applied research in the subprogram areas of economics, political science, sociology, law and social science, measurement methods and data improvement, and decision, risk, and management science.	NA	NA Applications are accepted at any time.

Contact	Description	Requirements	Funding
James Piereson, Executive Director The John M. Olin Foundation, Inc. 100 Park Avenue, Suite 2701 New York, NY 10017 (212) 661-2670	**The John M. Olin Foundation, Inc.** Supports research on the formulation, implementation, and evaluation of public policy in the social and economic field. Sponsors projects in the areas of economic policy studies, tax policy, strategic and international studies, political thought, law and economics, regulatory policy, fiscal policy, monetary policy, welfare policy and public interest law.	The applicant should submit a copy of the IRS letter confirming the organization's tax exempt status.	Ranges from $20,000 to $300,000. All requests are reviewed and acknowledged promptly.
Wyndham Anderson, Executive Vice President Pfizer Foundation 235 E. 42nd St. New York, NY 10017-5755 (212) 573-7578	**Pfizer Foundation Grants** are to accredited colleges and universities and specific departments within such universities.	All recipients must be registered with the IRS and hold 501(c)(3) nonprofit status. No grants to individuals.	Range from $1,000 to 500,000. Applications are accepted at any time.
Maureen P. Kingston, Secretary Price Waterhouse Foundation 1251 Avenue of the Americas New York, NY 10020 (212) 489-8900	**Price Waterhouse Foundation.** Supports professorships, fellowships, scholarship funds, research, employee matching gifts, annual campaigns, building funds capital campaigns, endowment funds, and general purpose funds which advance higher education in the field of accountancy.	No grants to individuals.	Average range from $1,000 to $20,000. Submit letter of inquiry and summary of proposal preferably before July.
Joanne B. Beyer, Vice President Scaife Family Foundation Three Mellon Bank Center 525 William Penn Place Suite 3900 Pittsburgh, PA 15219-1708 (412) 392-2900	**Scaife Family Foundation Grants.** Supports programs that address national and international public policy issues, education, health services and social welfare.	All recipients must be registered with the IRS and hold 501(c)(3) nonprofit status. No grants to individuals.	Range from $25,000 to $50,000. Applications accepted at any time.

(Continued on next page)

TABLE 3 (Continued)

Granting Institution	Title/Topic Areas	Eligibility Requirements	Size of Award/ Application Deadline
Richard M. Larry, President Sarah Scaife Foundation P. O. Box 268 3900 Three Mellon Bank Center 525 William Penn Place Pittsburgh, PA 15230 (412) 392-2900	*Sarah Scaife Foundation Grants Program.* Supports programs which are concerned with research and education in public policy and public affairs on a national/ international level.	All recipients must be registered with the IRS and hold 501(c)(3) nonprofit status. No grants to individuals.	Range from $1,000 to $875,000. Applications are accepted at any time.
Ralph E. Gomory, President Alfred P. Sloan 630 Fifth Ave. 25th Floor New York, NY 10111-0242 (212) 582-0450	*Alfred P. Sloan.* Supports general purposes, seed money, research, fellowships, conferences and seminars, and special projects in the areas of education, economics, and management.	No grants to individuals, or for endowment or building funds, or for equipment not related directly to foundation-supported projects.	Average range from $10,000 to $300,000. No deadline.
Marion M. Faldet, Vice President The Spencer Foundation 900 North Michigan Ave. Suite 2800 Chicago, IL 60611 (312) 337-7000	*The Spencer Foundation.* Supports research in the social and behavioral sciences offering promise of contributing to the improvement of education in one or another of its forms in the U.S. or abroad. The Foundation conducts a Small Grants Programs which is intended to facilitate scholars in pursuing exploratory, problem-finding, pilot, modest research projects.	No grants to individuals (except those working under the auspices of an institution).	Average range from $20,000 to $90,000. No deadlines.
Clement E. Hanrahan, Director The UPS Foundation Greenwich Office Park 5 Greenwich, CT 06831 (203) 862-6374	*The UPS Foundation Grants* support higher education in the area of public policy and transportation research.	All recipients must be registered with the IRS and hold 501(c)(3) nonprofit status.	Average range $2,000 to $50,000. March 31, September 1. Submit proposals January through August.